D1516215

CRITICAL GUIDES TO SPANISH TEXTS

2

Cervantes: Two novelas ejemplares

CRITICAL GUIDES TO SPANISH TEXTS

Edited by

J. E. Varey and A. D. Deyermond

CERVANTES

TWO
NOVELAS EJEMPLARES

la gitanilla

la ilustre fregona

*

JENNIFER LOWE

Lecturer in Spanish in the University of Edinburgh

Grant & Cutler Ltd

in association with

Tamesis Books Ltd

1971

Depósito legal: M.-12885-1971

Printed in Spain by Talleres Gráficos de Ediciones Castilla, S.A.
Maestro Alonso, 23 - Madrid

for

GRANT & CUTLER LTD,
11, BUCKINGHAM STREET, LONDON, W.C.2.

Contents

I Introduction   7

II La gitanilla   27

III La ilustre fregona   56

IV Conclusion   75

    Bibliographical Note   79

Acknowledgements

I wish to express my thanks to Professors A. D. Deyermond, A. A. Parker, E. C. Riley and J. E. Varey who, at various times and in various places, knowingly and unknowingly, have contributed to this book.

I

Introduction

Miguel de Cervantes' most famous work is, rightly, *Don Quijote,* a book which has been translated into numerous languages, adapted for films, ballet and, a doubtful honour indeed, even musical comedy. Although we can applaud and appreciate the success that this outstanding work has had it is perhaps unfortunate, albeit inevitable, that it should have tended to overshadow Cervantes' other work, both within and without Spain. For Cervantes is far from being a one-book man. Alongside *Don Quijote* (1605 and 1615) are to be found his pastoral novel *La Galatea* (1585), ten assorted plays, eight lively *entremeses* or short sketches, the collection of the twelve *Novelas ejemplares* and the lengthy, eventful story *Los trabajos de Persiles y Segismunda* (1617) as well as the customary quota of poems. If variety is immediately suggested by this catalogue, this impression is deepened when we look more closely at the works listed in it. At one end of the scale we have the rustic artificiality of *La Galatea* and at the other the bawdy jokes, the fast-moving dialogue and action in the sketch *El viejo celoso.* In between these two extremes we can find descriptions of life in slavery in Algiers or life in the inns of Castile, comments on contemporary literature, considerations on marriage, honour, love, freedom; the complete list would be a long one. In all this variety the common factor is Cervantes himself, whether it is Cervantes the reader, Cervantes the captive, Cervantes the observant traveller, or simply Cervantes the man. The first three categories obviously relate specifically to aspects of his life. In *Don Quijote* he tells us that he is "aficionado a leer, aunque sean los papeles rotos de la calle" (*Don Quijote*, I, 9) and, allowing for an element of artistic exaggeration, we can accept this as accurate, for his wide reading is obvious from the numerous references and reminiscences in his work. The five years spent as a captive of the Turks not only showed him another way of life but, we can assume, also brought him into close contact with human suffering. The routine job which he had arranging for supplies for the Spanish Navy entailed a vast amount of travel in Southern Spain and this clearly kept him in touch with everyday life and everyday people. Cervantes never lived and wrote in what later generations have come to call an ivory tower. His hypothetical dwelling could best be imagined as a caravan, well equipped with books and windows.

Since we are specifically concerned here with two of Cervantes' prose works we must first try to form some idea of the type of prose fiction with which he and his contemporaries would be acquainted. This particular literature falls neatly —maybe too neatly— into three broad groups of novels: chivalresque, pastoral and picaresque. The term 'novel' has been used here as it was earlier when referring to *La Galatea.* In using it we must always bear in mind that it does not and cannot denote all that the modern novel stands for. Many of these works appear very distant relatives of the nineteenth- and twentieth-century novel. At this time the terms normally used in Spain to denote lengthy works of prose fiction were *historia* and *libro,* the equivalent critical term in English being 'romance'. In this context *historia* must not be translated or understood literally but equated to 'story'. This, however, is unsatisfactory for critical purposes, as is *libro.* 'Romance' is potentially misleading in view of some of its popular modern connotations, although as a critical term it adequately defines the essential atmosphere of the chivalresque and pastoral works. It is not, however, applicable to the picaresque. Thus, in view of these considerations, I shall continue to use the term 'novel' simply because it is the most convenient all-embracing term. As summaries, labels and generalisations are often deceptive, frequently dangerous and always dull, it is a more useful exercise to read one representative text than to absorb the data contained in pre-digested paragraphs. However, since to study our texts in isolation would be equally deceptive, dangerous and dull, some indication of the literary background must be given. Cervantes did not write in a vacuum and so we must not create one.

The chivalresque novel held sway in Spain in the late fifteenth century and for much of the sixteenth. The modern reader, searching for meaning and form, will probably conclude that these novels are trite and lacking in artistic unity. He might even be tempted to describe such a novel as a literary snowball, accumulating more and more layers as it proceeds on an apparently erratic path. Such a description would be somewhat unfair since, although the novels do not adhere to an obvious structural plan, their ever-growing number of story-threads are usually successfully interwoven to produce an overall and cohesive pattern.[1] Moreover, when we analyse these novels and look at them in relation to the time at which they were written we can perhaps glimpse something of their original attractive- ness and the reasons for their great popularity. It is perhaps not too far-fetched to consider them as lucky-dip novels, stories in which there was something for everyone. Mystery-story addicts would find plenty to satisfy them, for nearly all of these novels have plots which involve the disappearance of an illegitimate son/daughter in, say, Chapter Two and his/her reappearance and recognition fifty or so chapters further on or even in the next volume. Disguise is often essential; mistaken identity frequent. The wanderings of the heroes over land and sea, in various parts of Europe and with an adequate number of nautical and terrestrial disasters, would appeal to another section of the reading public. Battles, jousts, duels, feats of skill, all contribute to the action of these novels. The female readers might

---

[1]The particular type of unity found in the chivalresque novel is discussed by Eugène Vinaver. *Form and Meaning in Medieval Romance* (The Presidential Address of the Modern Humanities Research Association, 1966).

not particularly care for these last aspects but they would find plenty
by way of compensation in the portrayal of men such as Amadís,
Esplandián (son of Amadís, who had a novel all to himself) or
Palmerín. And the particular fascination about these men would be
their love-life, for through all the adventures, the fighting, the travel-
ling, a unifying element is provided by the presence of love. If we
immediately assume that such a feature will automatically give the
novel lasting, universal meaning we shall be mistaken, for the love
that is here presented is one which is conditioned by the conventions
of society and literature of its day. It is, in fact, courtly love, the
term given to the expression of love which became prominent in
Provençal at the end of the eleventh century and was such a dominant
element in the poetry of the troubadours. Although, as Peter Dronke
has shown, many of the elements of courtly love are not exclusive to
this particular time and society but occur in earlier literature and a
variety of countries,[2] this type of love was peculiarly suited to the
current social set-up. Basically it is an idealising love in which the
lover continually stresses his realisation of the superiority of his
lady, the inspiration he receives from her and his obedience to her
every wish. This does not mean, however, that he is unaware of or
unmoved by her physical attractions. The poet's adoration is rarely
directed towards the girl of his dreams whom he intends to marry
but, with the necessary amount of secrecy and fictitious names, someone else's wife or a lady whom it is completely impossible for him to
wed. This situation becomes more comprehensible when we recall
that, at this time, marriage was, for the most part, merely a convenient
arrangement, a business contract drawn up between two families,
with scant attention being paid to the two people involved. Thus,
love and marriage were considered as two very distinct aspects of life

[2] Peter Dronke, *Medieval Latin and the Rise of European Love-Lyric,* 2 vols
(Oxford, 1965-66).

and this, in its turn, led to a situation in which it was often thought that true love could exist only outside of marriage. C. S. Lewis, indeed, believes that: "Any idealization of sexual love, in a society where marriage is purely utilitarian, must begin by being an idealization of adultery."[3] But, as we read the poetry, we realise that the fact that the love may be adulterous is virtually irrelevant to its expression. It is a practical circumstance rather than a moral issue.

At first sight the type of love presented in the chivalresque novel may not seem to tally with the description of courtly love given above. We notice particularly that the circumstance of adultery is often absent. On the contrary, marriage may be and often is the aim and achievement of the two lovers. Yet the essence and effect of the love are still basically the same. Secrecy continues to be vital since the love is often one of which the parents would disapprove, and in any case it is an effective dramatic device. The lover still swears and practises obedience to his lady and is inspired by her to prove his worth in constancy or feats of valour. On occasions the lady may even set the lover specific tasks to test him. Separation is a continual hazard and provides an obstacle to the love, and the intervention of rivals or the presence of jealousy are also testing situations. The initial source of the love is frequently the beauty of the heroine although reference to other qualities such as virtue and fidelity may be made. The love of these chivalresque knights and their ladies undoubtedly prevents them from being mere cardboard figures but it does not completely humanise them for the modern reader, as more often than not we are aware that they are just responding in conventional ways to conventional situations.

Thus we can see that the chivalresque novel combined the accepted canons of literary love with a story which would appeal to the

---

[3] C. S. Lewis, *The Allegory of Love* (Oxford, 1958), p. 13. The book was first published in 1936.

imagination and emotions of the readers. If we are left with the idea of a handsome anonymous knight galloping across France towards his lady-love in a Spanish castle, killing half-a-dozen enemies en route, getting lost in a wood and finally bumping into his own illegitimate son, we shall at least have captured the essential flavour of these novels. We must not forget that the chivalresque novel was the starting-point for Cervantes' own *Don Quijote*. The hero's mind has been turned by the hours he has spent reading the chivalresque novels in which he has implicit faith. And they are not only the starting-point but also the medium, for Don Quijote sets out to search for adventures in which he, like the knights of old, may prove his worth and serve society. The novel is simultaneously a parody and a criticism of the books about Amadís and his fellows. Cervantes' specific criticism of this type of literature can be found in *Don Quijote*, I, 6, 47 and 48. But, of course, the implications of the novel far transcend this purely literary aspect.

Towards the end of the novel, defeated and disillusioned, Don Quijote returns home, and since he has promised not to depart on any more chivalresque jaunts for the period of a year he decides he will while away the months by becoming a shepherd in order to "entretenerse en la soledad de los campos, donde a rienda suelta podía dar vado a sus amorosos pensamientos . . ." (*Don Quijote*, II, 73). In other words, instead of modelling his life on that found in chivalresque literature he intends to adopt the pattern found in the pastoral novels. Although he suggests equipping himself with some sheep the quotation given above shows that his pursuits are going to be cerebral and emotional rather than manual. In fact, Don Quijote's particular expression of his aims can serve as an acceptable generalisation on this branch of literature. The Spanish pastoral novel is rooted in a tradition which stretches right back to antiquity with the works of Theocritus and Virgil. Its more immediate ancestors are the Italian poems, plays and novels which are based on this theme and, within Spain, the plays of Juan del Encina (1468?-1529?) and Gil Vicente (1465?-1537?) and the eclogues of Garcilaso de la Vega (1503-36). We must not forget that at this time there were very close political and social links between Spain and Italy: indeed the Spanish Empire included certain parts of Italy. These links helped to bring Spanish authors into contact with the literature of the Italian Renaissance which had an unmistakable influence upon native Spanish literature, and not least in the sphere of the pastoral.

The world of the chivalresque novel was patently unreal because it contained so many incredible incidents; with the pastoral novel the sense of unreality stems chiefly from its artificiality. We are confronted with a tailor-made rustic setting in which the prime components seem to be grassy banks (for sitting on), streams (for listening to or weeping into), flowers (for picking), trees (for hiding behind or leaning against) and sheep (for the sake of appearances). Despite this basically functional rôle of the setting it may often be presented with skilful effect by the author, and its tranquillity may be used to contrast with other aspects of the story. Moreover, in theory, the natural setting is meant to convey also an idea of the harmony of the Universe, brought about by love (see below). The intention is that it should present in miniature the vastness of the natural Universe, that it should, in fact, be a microcosm. In practice, however, the settings often become so stereotyped in their design that this aspect ceases to be very meaningful to us. This rustic setting is peopled by unlikely shepherds and shepherdesses. One is often tempted to think that the majority of them could probably not tell one end of a sheep from the other. They are frequently accompanied by pseudo-shepherds and shepherdesses, in other words disguised escapees from the Court and/or unhappy love affairs. And what do they do? Virtually nothing. If the chivalresque heroes were characterised by excessive activity, their counterparts in the pastoral novel are remarkable for their inactivity. For the most part the only action that is recorded is in the past tense, presented as an accomplished fact and conveyed through the tales they narrate. By way of compensation they talk and sing day in, day out, and the subject of their conversations, stories and songs is almost always love and its attendant circumstances. Jealousy, disdain, hope, infidelity, beauty, physical desire, *desamor* (that is, lack of love) are all analysed in discussion or exemplified in the stories that are told. The influence of Italian literature, particularly the tales of Boccaccio as in his *Decamerone* (1353), is often noticeable in the stories recounted by these characters. But it is in the many discussions that a dependence on Italian sources is more clearly visible since here we often have a close adherence to the material of the Neoplatonic love treatises which flourished in Italy in the fifteenth and sixteenth centuries and which often became equally popular in their Spanish versions. This dependence ranges from vague reminiscence to word-for-word imitations. In its purest sense Neoplatonic love implies the conception of human love as the first step towards a realisation of divine love. Similarly, human beauty is considered as an accessible reflection of divine beauty. Both should be used as a means to a spiritual end. The basic idea is, of course, derived from Plato — hence the term Neoplatonism. But on to it have been grafted all the ideas on love of the intervening generations so that even courtly love, with its emphasis on the individual relationship as opposed to the universal implications of Neoplatonic love, is involved, contributing particularly the concept of the superiority of the lady. But this, like several other features, is now given a much more spiritual interpretation. The treatises to which the definition Neoplatonic can be most accurately applied are, then, those which discuss love, in all its varied aspects, as a means to an end. But since in human life love rarely occurs in isolation we soon find that its analysis and discussion become inseparable from a study of other human passions. Jealousy in particular was a prime favourite whilst the interminable attempt at differentiating between genuine love and physical appetite also occupied countless pages. Even now it is possible to appreciate the fascination that these treatises would have for contemporary readers, for the subtlety of many of their arguments (often in dialogue form), their wide coverage of the subject, the illustrative examples which are often included and the problems which are posed provide both intellectual stimulus and entertainment value. In including passages from these works the authors of the pastoral novels were linking their fictional presentations to contemporary thought on love. In his *Diana* (1559) Jorge de Montemayor includes almost verbatim a section from the Spanish version of León Hebreo's *Diálogos de amor*, whilst Cervantes' *Galatea* contains passages from Pietro Bembo's *Gli Asolani* and Mario Equicola's *Libro di natura d'amore*. These borrowings are not acknowledged: spotting the authors probably provided the readers with great enjoyment, one which is nowadays the preserve of the literary critic. Literary borrowing of this sort was commonplace in this era and, if it was done with the aim of embellishing one's own work, was considered commendable rather than reprehensible.

We must not get the impression that the pastoral novels are concerned mainly with theoretical and intellectual analyses of love. As implied earlier they also tell a story; or rather, stories. The plural is important, for in addition to the main story-line (the one about Diana or Galatea in the two books cited above) many other stories and situations are presented concerning other members of the pastoral community or the refugees from the outside world. The structure is usually complex with a growing accumulation of unresolved problems and half-finished stories. On the dramatic level this helps to create suspense; on the thematic one the various incidents and the different characters involved can thus be implicitly or explicitly compared or contrasted by their deliberate juxtaposition so that various aspects of, for example, jealousy or *desamor* are high-lighted. The very structure of the novel thus forces the reader to weigh up the respective claims of the lovers for sympathy or help. Poetry plays an important rôle in these novels, usually in the form of songs. Frequently they crystallise the emotion, suffering or hopes of a lover. Or they may be used to eulogise his beloved. Two-part songs are often in evidence, with either two lovers vying in their praise of their respective lasses, or else two rival suitors amicably harmonising their views on the lady concerned. Through the poetry, too, a close link was often established, in words or harmony, with the natural setting.

The chivalresque and the pastoral novels have in common an idealistic approach and presentation and only very occasionally does a glimpse of the real world intrude. The world created by these novels was one into which their readers could escape, not one which was identifiable with that in which they lived. Any similarity between the two worlds was to be found on the ideological level in the way in which these novels reflected the current fashions in love. When we turn to the picaresque novel we are faced with works which are very different in content, presentation and purpose. On the purely literary level we can consider the picaresque novel as the anti-thesis of its two predecessors. Here the world which is presented is one which bears a close similarity to that of sixteenth- or seventeenth-century Spain, even though the basic reality is often deliberately exaggerated or deformed. The characters we now meet are not the daring knights and beautiful damsels or the faceless shepherdesses and their swains, but hard-up noblemen, priests, beggars, school-teachers and, of course, the *pícaro* himself. In his recent study of the picaresque novel, *Literature and the Delinquent* (Edinburgh, 1967), A. A. Parker has pointed out that the usual tendency to translate *pícaro* by 'rogue' can be rather misleading since for us the word now has pleasantly mischievous connotations. He feels the term 'delinquent' more adequately conveys the frequently serious

nature and intention of these novels. It is perhaps helpful to let the
two terms co-exist in our minds.

The second basic difference between this type of novel and the
two already discussed is that of their viewpoint and attitude. Several
of the picaresque novels —particularly those that are the most
satisfying— give evidence of a desire to depict life in a serious and
responsible manner. Man's weaknesses, his pride, ambition, hypo-
crisy, self-deception or pettiness are all paraded before us. This
is not to suggest that the chivalresque and pastoral novels were, by
contrast, completely frivolous and irresponsible. There are, indeed,
some heavy-handed moralising passages in *Amadís de Gaula* and
some sententious comments on virtue in *Palmerín de Inglaterra.* The
incidents in the pastoral novels often illustrate implicitly or
explicitly the dangers of an excess of jealousy or disdain and Gil
Polo's continuation of the story of Diana, *Diana enamorada* (1564),
has a clear tendency to sermonising. Yet if all these passages and
comments were removed we should not immediately notice any
specifically serious intention on the part of the authors. Their main
concern would seem to be to give pleasure. The same cannot be said
of the main-stream picaresque novels. In Francisco de Quevedo's
Vida del Buscón (1603) the moral to be deduced is an integral part
of the story; in others, such as Mateo Alemán's *Guzmán de Alfarache*
(1599 and 1604) or the anonymous *Lazarillo de Tormes* (1554), a
precursor of the picaresque novel proper, the story serves to illustrate
the points that the author wishes to put over. This emphasis on the
serious message of many of the picaresque novels may give the
impression that they are books to be avoided when entertainment
value is desired. This is, however, a false impression. The picaresque
novels are guaranteed to make you laugh —producing real laughter,
not just condescending smiles— far more often than the chivalresque
or pastoral ever did. They are wittier, more ingenious, more gripping,
more vivid than their predecessors. Thus it seems that they are at

one and the same time more serious and more comic than the two types of novel we have already looked at. This apparently paradoxical situation is not as perplexing as might be thought.

First, the serious purpose. At the end of the sixteenth century in both Italy and Spain the moral responsibilities and qualities of literature are repeatedly stressed either in the works of fiction themselves or in the numerous didactico-religious works which were being published. The mere fact that literature should be seen to have a serious moral concern is not in itself remarkable nor unique to this epoch. But we are made aware of a particular emphasis on it at this time and this can be accounted for to a large extent by the attitude which was fostered by the Counter-Reformation and specifically by the deliberations of the Council of Trent in the mid-sixteenth century. Concerned to stop the spread of Protestantism in Europe, Roman Catholic leaders set up this Council in an attempt to decide how best they might counter what they considered the pernicious reforming zeal of the Protestants. It was in many respects a council of war, for the Catholics soon realised that effective resistance or attack could be accomplished only if they themselves were well-armed doctrinally. Hence there began a re-examination of their ideas and attitudes, often presented through serious treatises. But this attitude frequently percolated through to fiction as well, with many authors showing a far more responsible attitude than that of writers of previous generations. These authors were, moreover, aware that literature was becoming a more far-reaching medium and they realised its edifying potentialities (see E. C. Riley, *Cervantes's Theory of the Novel* [Oxford, 1962], pp. 95-6). Many of the picaresque novels, then, reflect the serious and responsible bias of literature at this period, though we must not make the mistake of thinking there is a sudden and clear-cut division between the writing of works of entertainment and those with a more educational intention. The obvious humour of these works is not just an optional extra nor solely an attempt to sweeten any moralising pill the author may be administering. Naturally, the humour does help in this respect but the reason for its presence is basically one of literary history and closely linked to the fact that these novels were purporting to portray real life, and usually low life. The classical theory of the 'Division of Styles' became of great interest in Italy and Spain in the sixteenth and seventeenth centuries. The literary theorists discoursed at length on all the various ramifications whilst the practical implications were shown in literature. The styles were three in number, each being known by two alternative names. There was the high or grand, the intermediate or mixed and the low or plain. Each style was considered appropriate for a certain type of literature or class of character. Thus the high style was reserved for tragedy, the expression of elevated ideas and ideals, noble characters and the like; the intermediate was applied to histories, general treatises and the pastoral (as a compromise between the high sentiments and the 'low' shepherds); whilst the last of the three was that thought fitting for comedy and the depiction of everyday life. Two or more styles might well co-exist within a single work as, for example, in a play, where the noble characters would speak in the elevated high style and a group of peasants would communicate in low style dialogue, often humorous in itself and by way of contrast. Thus, since the low style was intended for both the comic and the everyday, the two soon came to be equated. So when we laugh while reading a picaresque novel it does not prove that the works are just light entertainment. We laugh, but we stop and think as well.

Naturally, the lives of the *picaros* do not conform to any single pattern but some generally applicable biographical facts can be established. The *picaro* is usually forced to go out into a hostile world at an early age either because he is an orphan, or because his parents demand that he earn his own living, or because of ill-treatment. Thus he must devise methods for keeping himself fed and clothed. He will deceive, in word or action, steal, attack or betray, all to further his own ends. In outline such a career seems far from attractive. However, though it may be sordid, depressing, cynical, it brings a breath of fresh air after the stifling, enclosed world of the chivalresque and pastoral novels, even if the fresh air wafts along with it the smell of Lazarillo's regurgitated sausage.

Such, then, are the general characteristics of the Spanish prose fiction which forms the background to Cervantes' compositions: stories which were by and large closely related to the time at which they were written. Cervantes himself, as mentioned earlier, wrote a pastoral novel, although he never fulfilled his promise of finishing it; *Don Quijote* is rooted in the chivalresque tradition and includes stories with a pastoral background, whilst his tale of *Rinconete y Cortadillo* depicts a picaresque community. Yet Cervantes cannot be considered an author who merely followed an already established literary pattern. In the two works we are going to examine we shall see how he frequently re-interpreted traditional aspects of literature.

La gitanilla and *La ilustre fregona* form part of a collection of twelve short stories published in 1613 under the title of *Novelas ejemplares*. They were written at various periods before the date of publication and, with two exceptions, it is virtually impossible to assign dates of composition to any of the stories. The two exceptions are *El celoso extremeño* and *Rinconete y Cortadillo* which are found, in somewhat different versions, in a manuscript usually ascribed to the year 1606. In addition, *Rinconete y Cortadillo* is mentioned in the prologue to the First Part of *Don Quijote* (1605). Several critics have tried to deduce dates for the remaining individual stories either on the basis of internal data (references to people, events, buildings) or, with even less success, on the basis of maturity of style. The chief result of these investigations has been a series of conflicting dates for the *novelas*. Even more time and energy have been devoted to a consideration of the order of the *novelas* within the collection.

Casalduero, for example, states: "El orden de las novelas en la colección sí que debe preocuparnos, pues es claro que tenemos que suponerlo dispuesto por el autor."[4] With detailed explanations, he places the *novelas* in three distinct groups, with the middle one sub-divided, and in addition maintains that each *novela* has a thematic counterpart (pp. 25-7). He shows, too, how in each story a specific rôle is assigned to love and, though the importance of this rôle may vary, a unifying thread for the collection is thus provided. In his article 'Cervantes, El Pinciano and the *Novelas ejemplares*' (*HR*, XVI [1948], 189-208), W. C. Atkinson claims that, if *La ilustre fregona* were to follow instead of preceding *Las dos doncellas* "the sequence of the collection would show a regular alternation of new and exemplary with old and stereotyped" (p. 194). He believes that such an alternation was intended by Cervantes and that the order in which these two stories do appear is thus a technical error on the part of the printers. At the other end of the scale are critics like Ludwig Pfandl who categorically states: "Doce en número, aparecen dispues-tas por el autor sin obedecer a criterio ninguno y se suceden en pintoresco desorden."[5] Speculation of this sort is always entertain-ing; on occasions it may also be enlightening if it leads to a closer analysis of the works under consideration. But it is also dangerous, for close adherence to some such theory may end up by blinding one to other possibilities, implications and meanings. Although cross-references to other *novelas* are often illuminating, the need for an overall pattern does not really seem vital to our understanding and appreciation of the individual stories.

This collection of stories is prefaced by a prologue. The writing of such introductions was a common pastime for authors and this

---

[4] Joaquín Casalduero, *Sentido y forma de las 'Novelas ejemplares'* (Madrid, 1962), p. 11.

[5] Ludwig Pfandl, *Historia de la literatura nacional española en la edad de oro* (Barcelona, 1933), p. 334.

particular one by Cervantes is both revealing and helpful. He begins humorously by saying that it might have been better if his portrait had been stuck at the front of the book. As it is, he says, he must do the best that he can with words, and proceeds to describe his appearance. The first important point he makes is that all the *novelas* in the collection are very respectable stories. When love is presented it is done in such a way that there is no likelihood of any reader, careless or careful, being encouraged to get the wrong idea. It is all highly moral and Christian. This leads him on to the choice of the adjective *ejemplar* which, he claims, is very appropriate for "si bien lo miras, no hay ninguna de quien no se pueda sacar algún ejemplo provechoso". We still use the word 'exemplary', but in Cervantes' day it had a fairly specific meaning when used in a literary context for it implied 'containing an example or moral lesson', and was a term that was widely used in this sense in the Middle Ages when it was customary for both preachers and writers to extol moral and virtuous behaviour by means of anecdotes. He hints that, if he had time and space, he would point out to the reader the moral —"el sabroso y honesto fruto"— which could be extracted from each individual story and from the collection as a whole. He next switches the emphasis from moral benefit to aesthetic pleasure. What he has tried to do, he claims, is to provide a respectable, enjoyable form of entertainment which cannot possibly harm the participants. Recreation is essential for the good of one's soul. Gardens, parks, streams provide an opportunity for this and, in his opinion, literature is clearly an equally valuable form of relaxation. And if it is literature of a high standard it is, in addition, beneficial. He thus reverts to the exemplary concept, although he now stresses the negative rather than the positive side. For, having previously said that some specific good could be deduced from the stories, he now proclaims that if "la lección de estas novelas pudiera inducir a quien las leyera a algún mal pensamiento, antes me cortara la mano con que las escribí que sacarlas en público". Since, in his opening paragraph, he had told his readers that his other hand h'ad been useless from his warfaring days this would appear no light matter. The reason, he adds, is that when you have passed your sixty-fourth year (he was in fact sixty-six in 1613) you do not trifle with "la otra vida", by which he presumably meant that you do not jeopardise your own chance of salvation by encouraging your readers to stray from the path of virtue.

In brief, then, Cervantes is saying that these stories are meant to be enjoyed, that they provide the right kind of enjoyment and, in addition, a useful moral lesson. These two aspects are referred to by the writers of the *aprobaciones* which, as was customary, prefaced the book giving reasons as to why it should be published. The "honestísimo entretenimiento" provided by the stories is mentioned and it is claimed that the readers will be shown how to "huir vicios y seguir virtudes" and taught many "avisos y sentencias de mucho provecho". The need for the good intentions and moral tone of a work to be thus stressed was due partly to the fact that prior to publication, all books had to be submitted to the official censors. A system of censorship had functioned in Spain since 1502 and, with the spread of Protestantism, it became of increasing importance. The censors would decide whether or not the book lived up to the claims made for it in the *aprobaciones* and they were empowered to demand expurgation of any passages they considered detrimental to religion or public morals. If they considered the entire book to be potentially dangerous its publication could be prohibited and it was then placed on the official list of banned books, known as the Index. Thus, not only did an author have to try to make his book correspond to the required standards (which were admittedly somewhat inconsistent), but it was also in his best interests to advertise that he had done so. And in his prologue Cervantes is doing this at the top of his voice. Now, is all this stress on the exemplary nature of the stories merely an attempt to impress the censors or is it a real ingredient of the *novelas*? Cervantes certainly labours the point in his prologue so that the *novelas* seem whiter than white. Moreover, there were four *aprobaciones,* more than was usual, suggesting that Cervantes may have felt a little apprehensive about his chances of getting the collection published. As Riley indicates (*Cervantes's Theory of the Novel,* p. 102), he was probably mindful of the fact that the Italian *novelle* (see below) had a reputation for salaciousness and he did not want his stories to suffer from reflected immorality. Boccaccio, indeed, had been placed on the Index in 1559.

As was the case with the dating and the order of the *novelas,* the critics have found plenty to say about the actual presence or absence of *ejemplaridad* in them. Entwistle accepts Cervantes' own claims: "The exemplary novels have to do with moral doctrine. The author's words are too strong to be discounted as hypocritical or ironical."[6] Américo Castro's view of what he calls this "novelística confesión" is diametrically opposed, for he suggests that it was hypocritical of Cervantes to publish a *novela* like *El celoso extremeño* "después de tanto 'cortarse la mano' ".[7] Casalduero states that "Las novelas ejemplares no deben leerse para aprender algo, . . . no hay que buscar en ellas moral o moraleja de ninguna clase" (*Sentido y forma,* p. 54). But we soon come to realise that if he is unable to find what can strictly be considered a 'moral' he finds plenty of other concepts by way of compensation. The conflicting nature of these opinions suggests to us that the *ejemplaridad* of these stories does not immediately reveal itself with unmistakable clarity. In any event, Cervantes himself indicated in his words "si bien lo miras" that a search might be needed. In several of the stories the point that Cervantes is trying to make is obvious enough, either because he

[6] W. J. Entwistle, 'Cervantes, the exemplary novelist', *HR,* IX (1941), 103-09, p. 104.
[7] Américo Castro, 'La ejemplaridad de las novelas cervantinas', *NRFH,* II (1948), 319-32, p. 331.

explicitly states it or because the trend of the story and its resolution are such as to make the meaning very clear. For example, *El celoso extremeño* stresses the stupidity and the sin of a person's attempting to impose his will on another individual, whilst *La fuerza de la sangre* is an ultimately happy tale of virtue rewarded. Often, however, the 'example' has to be worked out by the reader in the light of the events of the tale. Cervantes might have said "si bien lo miras y remiras". And these 'examples' are not narrow, prudish morals but soundly based statements about life. If in his prologue Cervantes makes it seem as though the former were the case this is chiefly the result of his over-anxiety about the reception the censors would give his book. This is an extremely human tendency and even more comprehensible when we recall the situation which existed when he was writing.

Cervantes next moves on to another aspect about which he feels proud and which concerns the other term in the title of the collection: *novelas.* He tells us: "Yo soy el primero que he novelado en lengua castellana". The translation of *novelado* is crucial, for he means not that he is the first person who has written novels in Spanish —for that would be a preposterous and pointless claim— but that he is the first to have written short stories, for *novelas* is the word used to describe such works. As stated earlier, what we now call 'novels' Cervantes and his contemporaries described as *historias.* But even then it seems no small claim. Were there no short stories currently available in Spain? Cervantes himself goes on to point out that "las muchas novelas que andan impresas, todas son traducidas de lenguas extranjeras". Or, more precisely, from Italian, for at that time translations and imitations of the *novelle* of Boccaccio and Bandello were very popular in Spain, a popularity which, of course, the censors tried to discourage. Some of the stories included in *La Galatea* and some of the *novelas* themselves are Italianate in content and style, but the majority of them have a Spanish flavour and as Cervantes says, "mi ingenio las engendró y las parió mi pluma". So although we may feel that he is for a moment conveniently forgetting his own dependence on Italian short stories, although there is an obvious note of pride in his claim, the statement is one which is basically accurate, and, had he been able to foresee the future, Cervantes might have added that with his pen he had also marked out the guiding lines for the writers of future *novelas* in Spain.

In reading *La gitanilla* and *La ilustre fregona* we must be on the look-out for their *ejemplaridad* and must also consider the way in which the story is presented. Although we shall frequently find apsects which are still relevant today we must not expect twentieth-century attitudes and techniques to prevail. Moreover, we must not forget that some details which to us now seem hackneyed would be a novelty to Cervantes' readers, nor that what to us seems naive would, for them, often be profound.

II

La gitanilla

The opening lines of *La gitanilla* present us with the traditional picture of thieving gypsies (3).[8] Indeed, Cervantes seems to be particularly stressing this point since he uses the term *ladrones* five times in the first sentence, with *hurtar* being added a couple of times for good measure. Not a glimpse of any picturesque trait penetrates this apparently criminal scene. Casalduero feels that what Cervantes is here trying to do is to give the gypsies an "atributo tipificador" and that "el ritmo de la frase desposee a ladrones y hurtar de todo sentido peyorativo" (*Sentido y forma,* p. 68). Clearly, we are conscious of the stylistic effect of the sentence and well aware that Cervantes is exaggerating in his exclusive concentration on a single trait, yet the fact remains that the trait he has chosen is that of *ladrón* and our minds are conditioned by this opening sentence. Nor is there any relief in the second sentence when the "gitana vieja" is singled out as being particularly skilled in the "ciencia de Caco", a legendary bandit, and as having transmitted her skill and knowledge to her so-called grand-daughter, Preciosa. Up to this point we might be justified in thinking that we are about to read a story basically concerned with the underhand behaviour of the gypsy band, possibly with Preciosa conceived as a gypsy *pícara.* But the third sentence already starts to cast doubts upon any such expectations, for in the description of Preciosa we become aware that she is radically different from the gypsies mentioned so far. As her virtues are listed we immediately notice not only that she possesses an impressive array of

---

[8] All page references are to the Clásicos Castellanos edition of *La gitanilla* and *La ilustre fregona:* M. de Cervantes, *Novelas ejemplares,* I (Madrid, 1969).

skills and qualities, but also that these are all superlative in her. She happens to be "la más única bailadora . . . en todo el gitanismo" and, if this were not enough, "la más hermosa y discreta" not only in her circle but also in comparison with all those who lay claim to such highly prized titles (4). The harsh, outdoor life of the gypsies has never had any adverse effect on her complexion. If we found it difficult to accept Cervantes' initial concentration on just one trait of the gypsies, it is surely impossible for us to swallow this description of Preciosa. But, of course, we are not intended to accept all this as literally true, or even as feasible. Cervantes is here deliberately going to extremes of exaggeration in order to underline for us the vast difference between Preciosa and her fellows, a difference which is of vital importance for our understanding of the *novela* and which also reveals to us that she is "nacida de mayores prendas que de gitana" (4). Thus at the very beginning of the story Cervantes has revealed to us an essential detail about Preciosa. Moreover, the grandmother, too, is soon qualified as "abuela putativa" (6). Cervantes is clearly not intending to make a mystery of this particular aspect of the *novela*. We shall notice a contrast in *La ilustre fregona*.

By now we may have got the idea that what Cervantes is presenting is a seventeenth-century version of a conflict between the 'baddies' (the gypsies) and the 'goodies' (Preciosa). Moreover, even taking into account the artistic reasons for Cervantes' exaggeration of Preciosa, she may have seemed a little too perfect and Cervantes now tries to tone down this impression by telling us that "con todo esto, era algo desenvuelta" (4). But this *desenvoltura*, this touch of shamelessness in her, is not sufficient to affect her general high standards of *honestidad*. Indeed, as we discover later, it almost comes to be an additional quality in her since it is exploited so wittily.

The two qualities of *discreción* and *honestidad* with which Cervantes endows Preciosa may need a little elucidation, since literal translations of them are very misleading. By *discreción* we are to understand a balanced combination of intelligence, common sense and sound judgement, coupled with an ability to express oneself in an effective and, at times, witty manner. Similarly *honestidad* also embraces more than one attribute since it implies good behaviour, modesty and purity, the latter often having the particular connotation of chastity. Thus we can see that these are both major virtues and that Preciosa must, indeed, have attained the pinnacle of perfection if she possesses them to the high degree indicated by Cervantes.

Since the grandmother wants to exploit Preciosa's beauty and talents she is officially launched into Madrid society at the age of fifteen in an attempt to earn money by her singing, fortune-telling and, not least, her beauty. Cervantes gives us a very detailed description of this first public appearance. We are told of the day on which it occurred, of the number of people who took part in the dances, of the musical instruments that were played. In a comparatively brief description Cervantes conveys both the atmosphere and visual effect of the scene and in the midst of all this "la gitanilla" excels —this being the first occasion on which this name is given to her (7). Not only does she excel; she is also the physical centre of attraction for the crowd. With the balanced phrasing of "corrían los muchachos a verla, y los hombres a mirarla" we are enabled to visualise the way in which admirers rush continuously from all directions to gaze at this outstanding girl. Although Cervantes has been successful in the creation of this vivid scene he appears to feel it defies further description and when referring to her singing resorts to an expressive "¡allí fue ello!", leaving any additional embellishment to the stimulated imagination of the readers (7). However, he comes back into the picture when recording audience reaction to Preciosa's rendering of the song dedicated to St Anna. The comments are far from being in keeping with the religious nature of the poem and serve to emphasise the physical attractiveness of Preciosa as well as reminding us that she is merely a gypsy by adoption, for the exclamation " ¡Lástima es que esta mozuela sea gitana!" is nearer the truth than the audience realises (9). After this highly successful début in which Preciosa's superlative talents have been seen in action, the fact that she felt "algo cansada" is a nice human touch which brings her within the reach of the readers (10).

Her return to Madrid is again portrayed for us by means of several details which, although in themselves insignificant, together add up to a convincing picture. She goes back a fortnight later, with three other girls, and with a new selection of songs and dances. They dance in the shade in "la calle de Toledo" (10-11). More than two hundred people gather to watch and Preciosa's grandmother quickly fills her collecting box with coins. One of the minor town officials, the *Teniente,* passes by and in order to explain to us the reason for his subsequent actions Cervantes comments, in an apparently casual fashion, "que era curioso" (17). However, he is also concerned to preserve his official dignity and, not wanting to be a common by-stander, listens to only half the song and then instructs his servant to invite Preciosa to the house (17-18). The dramatic rôle of the *Teniente* in the story is virtually insignificant, but by means of a couple of revealing human touches Cervantes has made his brief appearance that of an individual. The two comments tell us something about the *Teniente,* but they do, of course, tell us far more about Cervantes and his approach to his writing.

Throughout the story we are to have examples of Preciosa's sound common sense and at this stage it is manifested to us in her answer to the gypsy girl Christina who is unwilling to enter a room where several men are gambling. Preciosa comments that "de lo que te has de guardar es de un hombre solo y a solas, y no de tantos juntos" and, in any case, "la mujer que se determina a ser honrada, entre un ejército de soldados lo puede ser" (20). This is an attitude similar to the one shown by Costanza in *La ilustre fregona.* But it is not only practical common sense that Preciosa shows; those who listen to her are continually impressed by her *discreción* and *donaire*. She shows a discerning mind and expresses her ideas in a witty, effective manner. The projected visit to the *Teniente*'s house takes place and brings yet more acclamation for Preciosa. Once again Cervantes creates for us a vivid scene. Doña Clara and her maids are all agog to see Preciosa and the other gypsy girls whose visit is eagerly awaited. Balance is again evident in the visual effect portrayed: "unas la abrazaban, otras la miraban, éstas la bendecían, aquéllas la alababan" (25). The resulting picture may be rather stylised but it successfully conveys the intensity and unanimity of the admiration. Their exaggerated eulogy of Preciosa's appearance is followed by a nice anticlimax when after a frantic search they have to admit that, between them, they have not a single coin Preciosa can use in her fortune-telling. Some humorous bargaining takes place and in view of "la esterilidad de la casa" they finally settle on a silver thimble (29). When Doña Clara's husband later returns home it is discovered that his pockets, too, are empty (32). Despite their dignified position and their ability to command the gypsies to perform in their house these gentlefolk are living in penury. Their social exterior is deceptive. It is not an aspect which Cervantes develops here but he has provided us in passing with a pleasing insight into a certain sector of society. The fortunes are told in verse which gives them added zest and prevents them from being taken too seriously. In the midst of the nonsense and the padding there are one or two sly comments which are meant to bear out the fact that Preciosa is "algo desenvuelta". Doña Clara, for instance, is warned to be careful of falling, particularly flat on her back, a position which would presumably be liable to produce more than mere bruises (31). After further witty dialogue the gypsies leave to return to their encampment and, with yet another nice touch of detail, Cervantes points out how they join a group of country girls who are making their way back to their village homes. Thus they are able to travel unmolested. Preciosa's earlier comment on safety in numbers (20) is thus presented from another standpoint (35). There is really no need to mention this incident since it has no dramatic value in the story at all. However, by including it, Cervantes has once again added perspective to the little world he is creating.

Up till now nothing has really happened in the *novela*, apart from the social launching of Preciosa. We have witnessed a presentation of her personality, we have been given hints about her background, we have been immersed in the colourful, melodious gaiety of the gypsy life. If anything is going to happen in the *novela* the moment is now due. Thus, as soon as we start the paragraph which states: "Sucedió, pues, que la mañana de un día que volvían a Madrid . . ." (35), our minds are alerted to expect that the story proper is about to develop. A handsome and obviously wealthy young man arrives and requests a private conversation with Preciosa and her grandmother. Are we about to learn something of Preciosa's real background? Is this a long-lost brother? And then the young man makes a speech. There is no other word to describe it. He presents his case, in elegant, studied prose. Whilst we cannot imagine any young man actually talking in these terms and this style to a gypsy girl, this manner of presentation serves as a means whereby the youth's good education, seriousness of purpose and sound character are transmitted to us. A somewhat different impression would have been caused if he had spoken in a more colloquial fashion. The young man is, in fact, madly in love with Preciosa and keen to prove his love to her, but he communicates this by means of several clichés. He claims, for example: "sólo quiero servirla del modo que ella más gustare; su voluntad es la mía" (37). His heart is like wax, she can stamp on it anything she wishes and he will preserve it as if it were inscribed on marble (37). It is all very formal and stylised. It might be almost any sixteenth- or seventeenth-century lover addressing his lady. But we must bear in mind the surprising fact that this is a young nobleman who is talking to and about a gypsy girl. Moreover, one of the points he stresses is that he intends to marry Preciosa. Now, we might well think that this was merely good tactics on his part and intended to make Preciosa and her grandmother well-disposed towards him. It would hardly be politic to come along and say "I intend to seduce and then abandon Preciosa". After all, even Tirso de Molina's Don Juan made a promise of marriage to some of his victims. There is, however, a comment which may make us believe that he is sincere. He begins his speech thus: "Yo vengo . . . rendido a la discreción y belleza de Preciosa" (36). He names two sources for his love, and this, and the order in which he places them, makes it seem unlikely that his is merely physical desire sparked off by her beauty. In Cervantes' *La fuerza de la sangre* the irresponsible young Rodolfo, suddenly struck by the beauty of Leocadia, drags her away from her parents during their evening stroll and rapes her before she comes round from a faint. This accomplished, his interest in her is at an end and it is only years later, after a series of coincidences, that they meet again and he is forced to make amends by marrying her. His was purely physical desire produced by physical beauty. He had no occasion and no urge to discover whether or not she had any other qualities. Preciosa's lover, on the other hand, shows that although he is not blind to her beauty, her character, as far as he is able to know it, is equally attractive to him. This, then, is a hopeful sign.

In the course of his proclamation of his love the youth reveals his identity to Preciosa and her grandmother: "Mi nombre es éste —y díjoselo—; el de mi padre ya os le he dicho; la casa donde vive es en tal calle, y tiene tales y tales señas" (37). The information is, however, kept from us at this stage. Presumably by doing this Cervantes wanted his readers to imagine that the concealed name was in fact that of a well-known *caballero* of their day. It is doubtful whether he really thought they would be deceived by this device. In any case the lad's real name is later revealed to us. Cervantes presents Preciosa's reply to her suitor in the same vein and style as his initial speech. This is meant to be a demonstration of her wisdom and intelligence, for as her grandmother says, when giving her permission to answer the youth, "yo sé que tienes discreción para todo" (38). However much we may be impressed by her logical and eloquent expression of ideas, Preciosa as a person really fades from the picture while it is in progress. Her naïve reference to her age, which should doubtless make her *discreción* seem all the more impressive, serves chiefly to widen the credibility gap. We see why Cervantes has done it in this way but the strain on the imagination is too great.

Preciosa is working on the basis that her ardent suitor is motivated chiefly by physical desire. She sees the danger inherent in this situation and her description of the likely outcome is very reminiscent of definitions in the love treatises mentioned earlier. Preciosa states: "sé que las pasiones amorosas en los recién enamorados son como ímpetus indiscretos que hacen salir a la voluntad de sus quicios; la cual . . . desatinadamente se arroja tras su deseo, y pensando dar con la gloria de sus ojos, da con el infierno de sus pesadumbres. Si alcanza lo que desea, mengua el deseo con la posesión de la cosa deseada, y . . . se vee ser bien que se aborrezca lo que antes se adoraba" (38). In León Hebreo's *Diálogos de amor,* for example, qualities of physical desire, *apetito*, are defined thus: "Tienen . . . estas cosas deleitables tal propriedad que, habidas que son, así como cesa el deseo de ellas, cesa también las más veces el amor y muchas veces se convierte en fastidio y aborrecimiento" (León Hebreo, *Diálogos de amor* [Colección Austral, Buenos Aires, 1947], p. 25). The readers of Cervantes' day would be well versed in such definitions. Moving from the general to the particular, Preciosa next places great stress on her virginity which she will yield only in marriage (39). The rose image which she used to convey how virginity can so easily be lost is at one and the same time effective and moving, and all the more so because, as A. K. Forcione points out, it is a striking inversion of the traditional flower motif found so often in lyric poetry, urging the reader to enjoy life while he is able to.[9] The inversion becomes even more meaningful to us when we recall that the best known English example, "Gather ye rosebuds while ye may . . .", comes from Robert Herrick's 'To Virgins, to make much of Time'. Despite her earlier admonitions she accepts his offer of marriage provided he accepts her conditions. The two-year gypsy apprenticeship which she demands of him will allow them to get to know each other and will also give him the opportunity to change his mind if he so wishes. Moreover, this challenging request will immediately determine whether or not his claims that "su voluntad es la mía" are really valid. The youth is momentarily stunned. As he says, he had never visualised anything like this (41). Doubtless his mind was running along literary lines. Maybe he saw himself as a latter-day courtly lover, demonstrating his prowess and fidelity to the lady of his dreams in an impressive, but genteel, manner. Or, at the most, performing daring feats like a chivalresque hero. Roughing it with the gypsies had not figured in his plan. However, he rapidly recovers his poise and, rivalling Preciosa's business-like attitude, shows he is ready to start his probation. Then, presumably encouraged by Preciosa's interest and approval, the youth feels emboldened to make a request of her: that she should refrain from going to Madrid where her beauty might attract others (41). This proves to be a false step. Preciosa refuses to have her freedom restricted and, in any case, if he is to enter into a relationship with her he must decide to trust her. Jealousy, as Cervantes demonstrates on countless occasions, is often a sign of lack of faith rather than great love and to *pedir celos*, to accuse the beloved of loving someone else, particularly at the start of the relationship, is either plain stupid or presumptuous (42). This reference to jealousy is the start of an important aspect of the *novela*.

[9] Alban K. Forcione, *Cervantes, Aristotle and the 'Persiles'* (Princeton, 1970), p. 311.

Preciosa's oration has been heavy going —for the reader as well as her admirer. We may have forgotten that the backcloth for this is the gypsy community. It is recalled to us by the lively interruption of the grandmother, whose concern with money shatters the rather academic atmosphere. We should note as a good sign that Preciosa's reasoning appears to have increased rather than diminished her suitor's passion (48). She, too, is genuinely attracted to Andrés (as he is to be known) but the motivation is *benevolencia* rather than full-blown *amor* (48). However, it is certainly a start, and in the right direction, too. Andrés is, as he feared, not the only one to be attracted to Preciosa for, under the guise of his literary interests, the poetry- writing page who has previously handed her a flattering poem (21-3) is also keen to win her affection. Preciosa and poetry virtually merge in his definition of his art, for the adjective *retirada* is the only term not really applicable to the girl (49).

The double-talk which takes place during Preciosa's pointed enquiries in Andrés' father's house allows us to see she is basically in favour of him and his plan. Moreover, by foretelling an imminent journey for him she facilitates his absence from home. In an idiomatic fashion she repeats an earlier warning to him: "Mira lo que haces primero que te cases" (55). All seems to be going well when, by chance, Preciosa drops the sonnet which the page has recently pressed upon her and it is read out by one of those present. In exaggerated and at times cliché-ridden language the sonnet tells of the devastating effect of Preciosa's great beauty and musical skill. The poem is melodious, owing in no small part to the abundance of the vowel 'a'. Once again we forget Preciosa's gypsy garb and share in the page's elevating experience when confronted with her beauty and superb singing. Andrés, who has already shown a tendency to jealousy, now nearly faints because of his fear of losing Preciosa. With a sudden change of style and presentation Cervantes addresses himself directly to Preciosa and her companions, calling their attention to the situation (59-60). Casalduero considers this an example of Cervantes' skill in so transforming reality into art that he "se siente no ya como creador, sino como mero agente de estas figuras que tiene delante" (*Sentido y forma*, p. 61). This suggests a subconscious process whereas Cervantes is here fully aware of what he is doing. He has momentarily halted his story and enabled us to see Andrés as Preciosa herself would see him. The general effect is that of a vivid tableau. With a few well-chosen words of advice Preciosa restores Andrés' equilibrium. This section of the story closes with further financial matters: again we see Cervantes' close attention to detail as he explains how the doubloon is shared out among the gypsy girls (63).

"Llegóse, en fin, el día que Andrés Caballero se apareció una mañana . . ." (63) and reading this we know that the next important stage of the story is about to follow —the start of Andrés' apprenticeship. He is greeted by "diez o doce gitanos" (64). Once more this is a nice touch of detail. It is, of course, irrelevant to the development of the story to know exactly how many gypsies were present. However, with the pleasing vagueness indicated by 'ten or twelve' Cervantes is almost teasing his readers. He, after all, is the creator of the scene so he, at least, ought to know. By his indecision he once more tries to suggest to us that it is reality he is portraying and that he, like any normal human spectator, is unable immediately to ascertain the exact number in the group. The cunning of the gypsies is revealed by their plans to transform the appearance of Andrés' mule whilst the strange induction ceremonies to which he is subjected present the type of activities one imagines gypsies indulge in. These are a suitable prelude to the speech in which one of the senior gypsies declares his intention of handing over Preciosa to Andrés. His words provide the most complete description of gypsy life found in the *novela* but it is at times a puzzling picture. His opening comments suggest an ideal society. Andrés is to be allowed freedom of choice in his marriage but he must accompany it by a pledge of fidelity to the one he selects. This is a tenet of gypsy life and means they are free from "la amarga pestilencia de los celos" (67). An admirable society indeed. Adultery is non-existent; incest abounds. If a tendency to adultery is discovered the gypsies execute justice themselves. And execute is the operative word. The model behaviour of their wives is a product of fear and not of mutual love and respect: it is a society organised for the benefit of the males. Their marriage laws also involve an elementary system of divorce in which a young husband can abandon an old wife in favour of one more his own age. And how did he come to be married to her in the first place? Apparently as a result of the matrimonial lottery: "queremos que cada una sea del que le cupo en suerte" (68). An admirable society? Praise for all the benefits of nature is soon followed by a description of the thieving activities of the gypsies and their ability to resist torture. The gypsy points out how their life is free from all the suffering caused by honour, ambition, favour-hunting and the like, for "nos contentamos con lo que tenemos" (70). On the surface this is an expression of an enviable state but when we pause to remember some of the things that *tenemos* embraces, our opinion will probably need modification. Throughout the speech Cervantes seems to be taking pleasure in steering an at times baffling course between the ideal and non-ideal aspects of this society. Many of the aspects the gypsy considers praiseworthy are shown to be somewhat dubious. Preciosa is forthright in her condemnation of their marriage laws. For her, marriage is a till-death-us-do-part relationship (72). Consequently, she repeats her earlier warnings to Andrés of the 'marry in haste, repent at leisure' variety. In all her actions she is going to be governed by her *voluntad*, her freedom of choice (71). Her body may be assigned to Andrés but she maintains the right to preserve the independence of her mind and spirit, her *alma*. This, then, and not the freedom desired by the gypsy, is the one we should classify as ideal. Contrary to our expectations, Andrés himself does not make a speech. He merely repeats his submission to Preciosa's demands and asks for a month's leave-of-absence from stealing to enable him to take some necessary lessons (73). The bubble of ideas and ideals is burst; humour has dispersed the froth of pompous oration. Moreover, the ensuing dialogue suggests that the opening sentence of the *novela* is, after all, going to be relevant. There is great jubilation when Andrés hands over some money as compensation for his expected loss of illegal earnings. He and Preciosa are enthusiastically cheered, a situation which makes some of the girls envious, for envy, Cervantes tells us, lurks in rustic hovels as much as in palaces (76). The old gypsy would doubtless not agree.

Having brought Andrés so far Cervantes now pauses and, as it were, reviews his situation, presenting the transformation in his life in a way calculated to make his behaviour seem unbelievably mad. It is, Cervantes points out in a welter of rhetoric, the result of love (77-8). The following scenes reveal to us exactly what sort of life Andrés has embraced. However, the thieving activities of the gypsies are described in a way that makes them seem like escapades rather than serious crimes. Andrés reconciles his own conscience with the gypsies' demands by purchasing his loot and appears such a first-class thief that Preciosa, "viendo a su tierno amante tan lindo y tan despejado ladrón", is delighted with his progress (79). After all, she is a gypsy by education if not by birth. Cervantes devotes but little space to the growth of love between Preciosa and Andrés. He merely informs us that "pasaba Andrés con Preciosa honestos, discretos y enamorados coloquios" which stimulated love in both of them (80). If we feel initially that Cervantes has dismissed this element of the *novela* rather abruptly we may, on reflection, feel relieved that we have been spared a series of amorous set-pieces. Imagination is a good substitute. It is, however, important to notice that the dialogue is not merely *enamorado* and that, in addition, Cervantes points out that their love depends upon the appreciation of *discreción*.

Andrés is successful in everything, love is blooming but: "Sucedió, pues, que . . ." (81). We recall that identical words were used when Andrés first arrived on the scene. Moreover, the use of the preterite in this sentence jolts us out of the state of pleasant monotony induced by the predominance of the imperfect in the preceding paragraph. The nocturnal arrival of the mysterious intruder gives us further grounds for suspecting that something is going to happen. Rescued from the attacking dogs the visitor is tended by Andrés and another gypsy. Andrés notices that the visitor is gazing at Preciosa and at once attributes this attentiveness to her beauty (84). It is a point in his favour that he is not immediately filled with jealousy. However, when Preciosa reveals that the youth is the poetry-writing page his worst suspicions are aroused and he believes the arrival of the lad is motivated by love of Preciosa, judging the page's behaviour by his own. We sense the possibility of plot complications. Andrés' reaction is criticised by Preciosa for she considers it indicates lack of trust on his part and reflects badly on her character; moreover she fears that "nunca los celos . . . dejan el entendimiento libre para que pueda juzgar las cosas como ellas son" (86). The jealous person gets things dangerously out of focus. The supreme example of this in Cervantes' work is *El celoso extremeño* in which the story stems from the distorted vision of life of a jealous old man.

Andrés anxiously awaits daybreak in order to question the visitor. We, too, want to find the answer to various questions. Are the suspected plot complications about to emerge? Will the page turn out to be a rival lover or a long-lost brother? Andrés is almost convinced that he is face to face with a rival but Preciosa's reassuring comment "le obligaba a vivir seguro" (87). He overcomes his jealous suspicions in obedience to Preciosa, not of his own volition. The moment for interrogation arrives; Andrés questions the intruder about his identity and his itinerary "aunque primero le preguntó cómo estaba" (87). Again, a nice touch of detail. The "aunque primero" relegated to

the second half of the sentence hints to us that this polite question
is of secondary importance to Andrés. As, of course, it is. The
explanation is unconvincing; Andrés' jealous suspicions surge up.
Using several lies he persuades the page to tell him the truth. The
dialogue is excruciating for Andrés who is now "como difunto" (90),
now laid low by "otro susto mortal" (91). But he keeps his head and
is rewarded by hearing the page say he has not come there out of
love for Preciosa. Consequently, Andrés begins to recover his
"espíritus perdidos" (92). The page's story is presented concisely,
clearly listing the factors which produce the tragedy he describes.
We are shown the disastrous effects which can be produced by
jealousy —the passion against which Preciosa is continually warning
Andrés. The story tells, too, of the tragedy which can be caused
when freedom of choice in marriage is not allowed. Although it deals
with a world very different from that of the gypsy community, we
can see that there are various points of similarity. The sombre atmosphere of this story is soon dissolved by the grandmother's hilarious
account of the reasons why she does not wish to return to Seville.
The page, Clemente as the gypsies name him, travels with the gypsy
community and Andrés becomes his constant companion in order to
keep an eye on him. No conversation between him and Preciosa takes
place until a month and a half after his arrival (99). Another detail
of time, but this time one which creates an impression of unreality
rather than reality. This detail is included chiefly to shed light upon
the respective characters of Clemente and Preciosa. Despite this,
despite his continuous vigilance, and despite the earlier reassurances
of Preciosa and Clemente's own disclaimer, Andrés does almost allow
himself to be overcome by jealousy when he hears Clemente
enthusiastically applauding his behaviour and the way in which he
has been won by Preciosa's beauty. He makes no mention of his fears
to Preciosa and "no tuvo celos confirmados, más fiado de la bondad
de Preciosa que de la ventura suya" (101). We can see here an

important development in Andrés in that he has voluntarily suppressed his jealous suspicions, relying on Preciosa's innate goodness instead of concentrating on his own precarious position. He is still over-prone to jealousy but is not now dependent on a verbal reassurance from Preciosa "que le obligaba a vivir seguro" (87). The apprentice is learning.

The friendship of Andrés and Clemente is underlined for us by the balanced phrasing which Cervantes uses to introduce their equally balanced song of praise about Preciosa. We find them "sentados los dos, Andrés al pie de un alcornoque, Clemente al de una encina, cada uno con una guitarra . . . comenzando Andrés y respondiendo Clemente" (102). The tableau effect thus created, with the two youths artistically arranged in the landscape, must, of course, be appreciated from a stylistic rather than a realistic standpoint. It is a technique frequently used in the pastoral novels where the shepherds, trees and streams are woven into a pleasing pattern. In Cervantes' *La Galatea* there are numerous instances of the type of balance found here. The balance is continued in the song with its amoebaean construction, the last line of each verse providing the opening for the next one. Once again, extreme claims are made for Preciosa's beauty and virtue and these are conveyed through the exaggerated terminology used. If it were not for the context of the poem and for the references to the *gitanilla* it could be interpreted as a poem with a religious bent. In this, the poem is in the Neoplatonic tradition in which human love was considered as the first stepping-stone to love of the Divinity. Clemente refers to "la preciosa / Honestidad hermosa" (102), and this idea is developed in Preciosa's own song when she states "Por mayor ventura tengo / Ser honesta que hermosa" (104). The path she is determined to follow is one which leads heavenwards. And this is the gypsy girl who was pleased when her lover appeared to be "tan lindo y tan despejado ladrón" (79)! But as we have seen on countless occasions, we are not meant to consider either the gypsies in particular or the *novela* in general from a rigid standpoint of reality. This song and the "discretas razones" that follow enable Clemente fully to appreciate Preciosa's worth and thus realise that Andrés' behaviour is wise rather than foolish (105). These songs were introduced by the expression "Sucedió pues . . ." (102) which on two previous occasions has preluded dramatic developments in the plot. We may perhaps feel deceived when on this particular occasion poetry takes precedence over plot. However, soon the tempo quickens and the pleasant pastoral interlude is replaced by the intrigues of Juana Carducha.

Our attention is immediately drawn to the fact that she is described as "algo más desenvuelta que hermosa" (105). These two attributes are found also in Preciosa but the emphasis is very different. Moreover, la Carducha is clearly completely lacking in *discreción*. Just as Andrés was attracted to Preciosa and stated his case and plans to her, so now la Carducha, having fallen in love with Andrés, outlines her situation and intentions to him. The terse, business-like manner in which she expresses herself is far different from the earlier, elaborate speech of Andrés. The stylistic difference in itself is sufficient to indicate that she is devoid of *discreción*. She bases her proposal on marriage but Andrés is well aware that she would readily dispense with such a ceremony and he thus decides that the best remedy is a speedy departure in order to "desviarse de aquella ocasión que el diablo le ofrecía" (107). Earlier, in describing the way in which Juana falls in love, Cervantes states "la tomó el diablo" (105). Casalduero believes this scene is introduced "para que Andrés venza la lascivia" (*Sentido y forma,* p. 65), and Andrés' reaction does, indeed, lend credence to this view. Yet, when we look objectively at the situation, and bear in mind Andrés' personality, his firmly-based love for Preciosa and the patent brashness of la Carducha, the idea of a real temptation must appear somewhat watered down. Cervantes could have presented Juana as a real challenge to Preciosa, in which case the situation might have been considered as a symbolic triumph over lust; as it is, the incident chiefly illustrates Andrés' *discreción,* for "como discreto, determinó de poner tierra en medio" (107). La Carducha feels snubbed when Andrés makes preparations for departure. His disdain of her proposal forces her to resort to desperate measures. Cervantes, like many authors of his epoch, frequently presents the effect of disdain on the unsuccessful lover. It may spur him (or her) on in an attempt to overcome the resistance of the loved one. All sorts of methods may be used, some as mundane as persistence, some more picturesque such as that of the anonymous lady who fell in love with Tomás in *El Licenciado Vidriera* and, finding she was "desdeñada y, a su parecer, aborrecida", gave him a love-potion in a quince. In other circumstances disdain may force the offended person to avenge himself on the person once loved. In the *Persiles,* Rubicón feels disdained and slighted when his beloved Ruperta marries Lamberto. His desire to avenge himself on Ruperta is so great that he kills her new husband. The frequency with which the topic of disdain occurs in sixteenth- and seventeenth-century literature may seem rather monotonous, but it is worth realising that this varied treatment of the effects of disdain is frequently psychologically accurate. La Carducha is motivated both by a desire for revenge and by the urge to keep Andrés within grasping distance. The method she uses to detain him is ingenious, though not original. Casalduero links her actions with those of Potiphar's wife in Genesis (*Sentido y forma,* p. 65); M. Bataillon ('La dénonciation mensongère dans *La gitanilla', Bulletin Hispanique,* LII [1950], 274-76) mentions another possible secular source. We are reminded, too, of an incident in the *Persiles* when the beautiful Hipolita uses similar means to detain Periandro and Cervantes calls her "nueva egipcia". In spite of Casalduero's assertion that the Biblical parallel "eleva el rango de la escena, y por eso le otorga un volumen típico, de dimensiones colosales . . ." (*Sentido y forma,* p. 65), the incident can really be understood and appreciated without reference to such sources.

The discovery of the jewels which la Carducha has placed in Andrés' luggage and the consequent claim that he is a thief provoke an even more serious incident. A soldier both insults and assaults Andrés, giving him "un bofetón, tal, que le hizo volver de su embele-samiento y le hizo acordar que no era Andrés Caballero, sino don Juan y caballero" (110). Seizing the soldier's own sword Andrés quickly kills him. The gentle, sensible, non-robbing Andrés has suddenly become a murderer. But that is not really how we react to the situation. In fact, we really approve of his action, since in his violent reaction to the soldier's gibes and slap Andrés has proved that he is still a man of honour; that, despite his present garb and situation, he has not allowed his character to deteriorate. To slap someone on the face was considered one of the most offensive and provocative actions; one which a man of honour must avenge. And Andrés has risen to the occasion. Pleading later for Andrés' life, Preciosa herself points out that, in his reaction, Andrés has shown "la bondad de su ánimo" (112). Thus, ironical though it may seem at first, by the murder Andrés has proved he is still a real *caballero*. The reaction of the bystanders is vividly conveyed by Cervantes through the use of the infinitive and the rapid succession of various events is com-municated by the repetition of *aquí* (110). In addition, the emphasis and balance created by "creció la confusión, creció la grita" and "por acudir Andrés . . . dejó de acudir" (110), enable us to visualise something of this dramatic scene. Andrés, we note, is easily arrested because, instead of trying to escape, he attends to Preciosa; another point in his favour. The entry into Murcia with the crowd eager to see Preciosa and Andrés recalls the busy streets in Madrid at the start of the story. Preciosa's beauty is once again the subject of wonder and praise; the *Teniente*'s curiosity had led him to listen and issue an invitation to Preciosa and now the curiosity of the wife of the *Corregidor*, the local magistrate, brings about the visit of Preciosa to her house.

Since we have known from the very beginning of the story that Preciosa is not a gypsy by birth we are put on our guard and alerted for dramatic developments when the *Corregidor*'s wife nostalgically equates Preciosa's age with that of her absent Costanza (112). Preciosa now pleads eloquently on behalf of Andrés, stressing the fact that she is betrothed to him. It is as if the imprisonment of her suitor has made Preciosa realize how much she loves him. Andrés' fate is postponed while Preciosa's true identity is established by means of her 'grandmother's' confession, the recognition of baby clothes and jewels and the conventional birthmark. (It should, however, be added that the details about the two webbed toes on her right foot introduce an element of originality.) We never discover why the old gypsy stole the infant Preciosa. The confession and recognition scene are accomplished as swiftly as possible, the revelation of Andrés' real name follows almost immediately and we then return to the subject of his arrest which must now be considered in the light of these new facts. Indeed, Preciosa herself appears to take a different view of things now. Despite the fact that she has just spoken so warmly of her love for her 'husband' Andrés, we next find her stating that she has no really strong feelings for him (120 and 123). This may initially appear somewhat disconcerting and disappointing to us until we realize that we are meant to consider this apparently off-hand attitude as part of her *discreción* and virtue. She has been shown to us as Andrés' faithful fiancée; she must now also be seen to be her parents' dutiful daughter. Her words of submission reveal her desire to be obedient; her sigh indicates the real state of her emotion, a fact which fortunately does not escape her mother's attention (120).

Andrés is, of course, oblivious of all these dramatic developments and so, when the *Corregidor* questions him closely about Preciosa, he quite naturally jumps to the conclusion that his interrogator has fallen in love with the beautiful gypsy girl, for "los celos son de cuerpos sutiles, y se entran por otros cuerpos sin romperlos" (122). Jealousy and suspicion well up as a spontaneous reaction. But we notice how he immediately pulls himself together and, without revealing his anxiety, commends Preciosa and shows his complete reliance on her judgement. The Andrés we see here is far different from the youth at the beginning of the story who became jealous and critical at the mere thought that someone else might fall in love with Preciosa.

The build-up for the final dramatic scene now begins. As ever, Cervantes pays great attention to detail and atmosphere. Andrés is brought out of the dungeon at night and led to the *Corregidor*'s house "sin ser visto de nadie, sino de los que le traían" (124). A truism, maybe, but a detail which helps us to visualise the mysterious nocturnal trip. If we are expecting the marriage to take place, the ensuing scene will be somewhat anticlimactic since the priest refuses to conduct the ceremony until all the legal formalities are complete (125). The censors would approve of this attitude whereas they would probably have objected to any suggestion of a hastily arranged marriage. However, there is plenty of emotion by way of compensation.

The final paragraphs neatly tie up most of the ends; the uncle of the dead soldier is appeased with money; Clemente, who dropped out of the story some time previously, is discovered to be on the way to Italy. The penultimate paragraph records, with what Forcione describes as "the familiar, dynamic *veni-vidi-vici* series of preterites" (*Cervantes, Aristotle and the 'Persiles'*, p. 309), the arrival of Andrés' father and the celebration of the wedding. Coupled with this we have the clauses: "se renovaron los gustos, se hicieron las bodas, se contaron las vidas" (129) which, by their balance, help to underline the happiness and harmony. And, then, the words "Olvidábaseme de decir . . ." tell us how the luckless Juana Carducha who had, in fact, precipitated all these events with her intrigues, confessed and was forgiven. Thus the story can close with the emphasis once again on balance and harmony: "en la alegría del hallazgo de los desposados se enterró la venganza y resucitó la clemencia" (130).

The story of Preciosa and Andrés has meandered along until reaching its expected happy ending. The *novela* was, in fact, well under way before the story proper got off the ground. From time to time there appeared to be a possibility of dramatic complications but they were never fully developed. The intrusion of Clemente was never exploited as much as we probably imagined it would be. Throughout his stay in the gypsy community we keep expecting he is about to play an important dramatic rôle but the greatest surprise he does in fact produce is his silent departure from the scene. Forcione presents a very interesting interpretation of the rôle of Clemente in the story. He sees him, basically, as Cervantes' portrayal of the apprentice poet. His career is very similar to that of Andrés for "the two young men are borne as doubles on parallel quests, following the object of their desires into a strange world beyond the outer limits of society" (*Cervantes, Aristotle and the 'Persiles'*, p. 316). Whereas Andrés emerges triumphantly from his probationary period, Clemente's mission is not yet accomplished and he is forced to continue his lonely quest. In addition Forcione shows how Cervantes' literary theories are frequently exemplified in Clemente. The argument is both attractive and convincing but we must not forget that it is the human and dramatic rôle of Clemente that would probably make the greatest impact on the majority of Cervantes' readers. Another apparent failure to exploit a dramatic situation is demonstrated by the fact that we are told at the very beginning that Preciosa is not a gypsy by birth, a disclosure which somewhat lessens the impact of the discovery of her real parentage. The giveaway expression "sucedió pues . . ." alerts us before an important occurrence (with one memorable let-down). All this goes to show that to write a dramatic, suspense-riddled story is clearly not Cervantes' main concern.

Is it, then, to present a fascinating picture of gypsy life? A situation very similar to that of *La gitanilla* is outlined in *El coloquio de los perros*, another of Cervantes' *novelas*, where the dog Berganza, recalling the time he spent in a gypsy community, mentions a nobleman's page who fell in love with a gypsy girl who refused to return his love unless he became a gypsy and married her. This trite little anecdote is accompanied by a description of thieving activities of the gypsies, their deceit, the idleness of the women, and other such features. The fact that gypsies do not marry outside their own community is attributed to their reluctance to let their bad habits be discovered by anyone else! The picture here painted is a bleak and unattractive one. The opening of *La gitanilla* suggests a similar portrayal but, as the story progresses, we come to consider dishonesty and thieving merely as inevitable, and on occasion amusing, characteristics of the gypsies. After all, the popular opinion of gypsies was, and still is in some quarters, that they are a thieving lot. Side by side with this conventional aspect we have the version and interpretation of gypsy life given by one of the leaders of the gypsy community. If the gypsies seemed unlifelike before, this portrayal makes them well nigh incredible. Apart from a passing reference to the artificiality of the *ceceo* in gypsies, giving as the sole example Preciosa's rendering of *señores* as *ceñores* (19), Cervantes makes no attempt at differentiating their manner of speech from that of the other characters in the story. Nor does he over-exert himself to include picturesque details of gypsy lore, quaint customs and all the other traditional paraphernalia. Clearly, to write a *novela* portraying gypsy life, whether idealistically or realistically, was never one of Cervantes' main intentions. Moreover, the portrayal we do have is not entirely idealistic, since we see the flaws and the failings of their society. Nor, of course, is it entirely realistic because gypsy life was far more unpleasant and sordid than Cervantes conveys to us here. Amezúa y Mayo considers that the overall tendency toward idealisation of gypsy life stems from Cervantes' realisation that his creation of such a perfect being as Preciosa ran counter to the depiction of a gypsy community based on those he knew to exist in reality.[10]

If we seek realism in this *novela* we must look elsewhere. And it is, in fact, in the accumulation of the small details which we have noted, that we come closest to an expression of reality. These details are, for the most part, irrelevant to either plot, theme or character portrayal but they do serve to present the appearance of observed reality. Now, obviously, Cervantes is not describing something he actually witnessed. The apparent uncertainty over 'ten or twelve gypsies' (64) or the fact that Preciosa can lean on a certain *reja* because it happens to be a low one (19) are not to be taken as evidence that Cervantes realistically records reality. The inclusion of all these details owes more to Cervantes' creative sense than it does to any actual occurrence. Compare some sample sentences. To say: "The woman opened the door to the visitor" presents a basic set of undeniable facts. Add a couple of adjectives and an adverb and we might get: "The old woman slowly opened the door to the unexpected visitor." Our curiosity and sense of expectation are aroused. Change the adjectives and adverb to give: "The young woman quickly opened the door to the smiling visitor" and an entirely different train of thought is set in motion. Although it might initially be thought that the first of the three sentences is the most accurate portrayal of reality and that the other two are simply examples of artistic elaboration, this is not, in fact, the case. People are individuals and they do not act without reacting. Thus, the two expanded sentences come nearer to a portrayal of reality because they convey this to us. Artistic creation has brought about the appearance of observed reality, and simultaneously it has produced added interest. This is what Cervantes

[10] Agustín G. de Amezúa y Mayo, *Cervantes, creador de la novela corta española* (Madrid, 1956-8), Vol. II, p. 14.

achieved. He has given added perspective to his *novela* through the numerous little details he includes, made many aspects more convincing and greatly increased our aesthetic appreciation of it.

It seems, then, that we must conclude that *La gitanilla* is a pleasant, rambling story, lacking in any real dramatic impact and not placing any particular emphasis on the gypsies themselves. Readable, maybe, but, to our minds, probably not a very auspicious beginning for the collection of the *Novelas ejemplares*. Moreover, this title reminds us that another aspect of *La gitanilla* must now be considered: its *ejemplaridad*. The most obvious point of departure is Preciosa's character. Her good qualities, her virtue, her intelligence are repeatedly emphasised. We are told that she has not allowed herself to be tainted by close contact with gypsy life. She maintains the standards and ideals in which she believes even though these do, at times, run counter to those of her companions. The portrayal of such a high degree of virtue is, of course, a dangerous undertaking. The virtuous character may come to appear incredible and consequently have no real effect upon us. Indeed, Amezúa y Mayo's critical assessment of her in itself reveals this potential danger: "Cervantes tuvo la fortuna, el singular acierto de modelar en la protagonista . . . la figura más perfecta, más lograda y cautivadora de todas las suyas femeninas" (*Cervantes, creador* . . ., Vol. II, p. 14). We realise the inevitability of the use of superlatives. Cervantes was clearly aware of this and it is for this reason that he adds a measure of *desenvoltura* to prevent Preciosa from seeming too goody-goody. But, in actual fact, her engaging *desenvoltura* soon comes to be considered as yet another attractive feature in her. If we are eagerly searching for reality we shall again be disappointed. Preciosa's skin has never become weatherbeaten like that of the rest of the gypsies; her conversation, in both style and content, is rarely that appropriate to a fifteen-year-old nomad. Cervantes wants to tell us what an admirable lass she is, brimming over with *honestidad* and *discreción*, and he frequently does this by elevating her thoughts and manner of expression. Although an objective assessment will lead us to appreciate the character of Preciosa and realise its *ejemplaridad* it is quite likely that she is somewhat over-sentimentalised for our taste, that she is too sweet, far too pink and white, literally and metaphorically. But we must not let our latter-day approach entirely govern our attitude towards her. For the readers of Cervantes' day Preciosa would be a vast improvement on the Italianate shepherdesses or distraught damsels they had so often encountered in their novels. She would also be more aesthetically pleasing than most of the females in the picaresque novels. Thus, it is not too difficult to imagine that they would find her personality more satisfying and her *ejemplaridad* consequently more effective than we do today.

However, for them and for us the real *ejemplaridad* of the story seems to lie in another quarter. In our study of the *novela* we have seen the detailed attention that Cervantes pays to the career of Andrés and, in particular, to the ebb and flow of his jealousy. The two-year breathing space before their marriage demanded by Preciosa is claimed to be a period to give Andrés time to think things over and for him and Preciosa to get to know each other properly. But we soon realise it is much more than this. Indeed, Preciosa herself refers to it as his *noviciado* (73) and although it is not necessary to place as much emphasis on the religious connotations of the word as Casalduero does, yet in the light of all Andrés' experiences the word is a significant one. In the course of the story he is involved in a series of potentially testing incidents, starting with the page's sonnet and finishing with the *Corregidor*'s interrogation. These are not situations specifically engineered by Preciosa in order to prove her lover's worth: they arise fortuitously out of the interaction of the various characters in the story. We are well aware that in themselves they are minor incidents but we have been told from the beginning of the jealous susceptibility of Andrés and are reminded later that "Nunca los celos . . . dejan el entendimiento libre para que pueda juzgar las cosas como ellas son" (86). What may seem trivial to us is therefore of tragic proportions to Andrés. Thus, when he overcomes his jealousy and suspicions, whether as at first out of obedience to Preciosa or as later of his own volition, it is a noteworthy achievement for him. And the progression in his ability to overcome the jealousy is clearly marked by Cervantes. Although he came near to fainting when the page's sonnet was read he replies frankly and courteously to the *Corregidor*. Thus, when he ultimately marries his Preciosa, it is not merely to provide a conventional happy ending to the story. Andrés is being rewarded: he has proved himself her equal in character (and she, conveniently and appropriately, turns out to be his equal in status) and the marriage thus provides a conclusion which is satisfactory from the point of view of the theme as well as from that of the story. Jealousy was frequently a topic of discussion or an element in the plot in many plays and novels of the sixteenth and seventeenth centuries. Cervantes himself often uses it in this way as, for example, in *La Galatea*. Undoubtedly the manifestations of and comments on jealousy as found in *La gitanilla* throw light on yet more aspects of this standard theme. However, in this particular *novela* it is obvious that Cervantes is using jealousy as a means to an end: to illustrate Andrés' progress. In choosing jealousy as the medium Cervantes was picking on a literary topic with which his readers would be well acquainted. For us, too, although we may not be acquainted with all the literary background to the topic, it proves to be a satisfactory and convincing method since the portrayal of Andrés' jealous fears and reactions is psychologically acute. In so using jealousy Cervantes is infusing new life into an old topic. He does the same thing on a much larger scale with his treatment of the chivalresque in *Don Quijote* and, as we shall see, in a different way, in *La ilustre fregona*.

It is, however, possible to find even deeper significance in the *novela.* Casalduero, for instance, claims that, in the course of the story "Andrés ha vencido el mundo, el demonio, la carne, al hacerse gitano, no sentir celos por la presencia del Paje-poeta, y rechazar a la Carducha" (*Sentido y forma,* p. 65). He is imprisoned, awaiting death, but instead emerges to a new life and marriage. This basically spiritual interpretation of the *novela* can, as we have seen, be criticised in some of its details as, for example, the equation of the Flesh and Juana Carducha. Forcione points out that the harmonious conclusion also presents the reintegration into the social order of both Andrés and Preciosa. In addition, the world of the gypsies is now replaced by the civilised setting of Murcia. Because Cervantes wants to underline the idea of harmony and redemption even Juana Carducha is forgiven and, by its striking vocabulary, "the final antithesis —vengeance *buried,* mercy *resurrected*— imaginatively associates [her] destiny . . . with that of the protagonists as it implicates her in the ritualistic celebration of death and rebirth which lies behind the plot of the *Gitanilla*" (*Cervantes, Aristotle and the 'Persiles',* pp. 309-10). Although it is undeniable that there is both evidence and justification for such interpretations we must always be careful that they do not lead us too far from a consideration of the *novela* as literature and do not mask its relevance to normal human experience. The career of Andrés presents us with a victory over self, a character growth which is a meaningful *ejemplo* in itself.

It is generally assumed that Cervantes deliberately chose *La gitanilla* to head the collection of *Novelas ejemplares.* Whether this is so and whether it was written specifically to fulfil this function is a debatable point. As already mentioned, our sophisticated twentieth-century minds will probably not be completely entranced by the content and presentation. However, we can see that it fulfils Cervantes' requirements for a *novela ejemplar* as outlined in his *Prólogo al lector.* Entwistle calls it "a novel of honest recreation with only incidental doctrine" ('Cervantes, the exemplary novelist',

p. 108). Clearly, nowhere does Cervantes preach at us, yet it is obvious that the *ejemplaridad* is fundamental to the whole concept and execution of the *novela* and not just an optional extra. We have, in fact, a successful combination of "ejercicios honestos y agradables" and "ejemplo provechoso".

III

La ilustre fregona

Our study of *La gitanilla* was conditioned by the meandering course of the *novela* itself. *La ilustre fregona* lends itself to a somewhat different treatment. The plot can be summarised as follows: A boy runs away from home to enjoy an unrestricted life on the tunny fishing wharves. On his return home he persuades a friend to accompany him on a second excursion to the wharves but, before they reach their destination, the friend falls in love with a serving maid and consequently they both decide to stay in the inn where she lives. It so happens that the girl is the illegitimate daughter of the father of one of the boys (fortunately not the one who is in love with her). So, since she proves to be of equal social status, the marriage can take place and the story, which never looked like being a tragic one, has the expected happy ending. What, we may well ask, is exemplary about all that? Does it even add up to a good *novela*?

The title immediately presents us with an antithesis and one, moreover, which would be more noticeable and simultaneously more outrageous to Cervantes' contemporaries. How on earth could a *fregona* also be *ilustre*? For the adjective not only conveys the idea of fame and distinction but also hints at high social rank. The curiosity of the reader would be aroused by this paradoxical title more than by the plain statement of *La gitanilla*. (A similar effect is created by the paradox of nationality suggested by the title of *La española inglesa*, another *novela* in the collection.) This initial antithesis persists throughout the story until it is resolved by the revelation of the *fregona*'s real parentage. The likelihood of Preciosa's real identity being disclosed was made clear to us at the very beginning of *La gitanilla*; no such hints are to be found in *La ilustre fregona*, though it is possible that some readers, particularly those well-versed in current literature, might have their suspicions from the outset. Let us assume, however, that ignorance prevails; it certainly increases enjoyment. The fact that the paradox of the title remains with us for virtually all of the story provides a unifying dramatic thread for the *novela*. Moreover, we find that the whole story has what can best be described as an antithetical structure. To recall the definition of antithesis as found in the *Concise Oxford Dictionary* may be useful: "Contrast of ideas expressed by parallelism of strongly contrasted words." It is not surprising, then, that in addition to contrast we are aware of a strong sense of balance.

Balance, indeed, predominates in the opening paragraph with the description of the fathers and sons: "el uno se llamaba don Diego de Carriazo, y el otro, don Juan de Avendaño. El don Diego tuvo un hijo, a quien llamó de su mismo nombre, y el don Juan otro, a quien puso don Tomás de Avendaño" (221). And it is in the presentation of the two boys that we are to find the greatest use of antithesis and balance, on a variety of levels. However, before their joint career begins, the emphasis is placed on Carriazo junior and we learn of his grief when he finally decides to leave the fishing wharves and return home: "dejó con ellos la mitad de su alma, y todos sus deseos entregó a aquellas secas arenas" (228). Andrés left Preciosa after his declaration of love and "enviándole con la vista el alma, sin ella . . . se entró en Madrid" (48). La Carducha, seeing Andrés depart, felt that "se le iba la mitad de su alma" (107). In other words, what Cervantes is here doing is describing Carriazo's attitude to the wharves by means of the language of love. The clichés which were used in conventional circumstances in *La gitanilla* are here being used in a most unorthodox fashion. On his return home he mopes about like a lovesick person, unable to find interest in anything (229). Avendaño, aware that his friend is pining, "se atrevió a preguntarle la causa, y se obligó a remediarla . . ., con su sangre misma" (229). Presumably he imagined

Carriazo was thinking nostalgically of a girl he had left behind him. And, in fact, Cervantes has presented the whole situation from this standpoint. His purpose will become clear later.

The account of Costanza's beauty overheard by the two lads impresses both of them: "especialmente a Avendaño, en quien . . . despertó . . . un intenso deseo de verla. También le despertó en Carriazo; pero . . ." and the *pero* introduces the comment that, despite his curiosity, the fishing wharves have a greater pull on him (239). Avendaño is attracted —admittedly by hearsay— by a girl; Carriazo by the wharves. On reaching the inn where the girl is known to live, Avendaño stations himself at the door and Carriazo, unable to drag him away, keeps him company. However, their wait is destined to be a long one. "Entrábase la noche, y la fregona no salía; desesperábase Carriazo, y Avendaño se estaba quedo" (240). The whole sentence is a beautifully balanced one, this effect being achieved by the double inversion: verb-noun/noun-verb; verb-name/ name-verb. This balance is far from being fortuitous. In the first part of the sentence it is intended to reinforce the humour which arises from the incongruity of linking the advance of night with the non-appearance of the wench. The verbs *entrar* and *salir* form a recognised pair; the nouns *noche* and *fregona* do not. Where the two lads are concerned, although they are superficially balanced, we see that in their attitudes they are straining to break this balance. However, as later becomes apparent, they are more similar than the present situation might suggest. Thus the stylistic technique here employed by Cervantes is one which gives added meaning to the statements he is conveying.

Patience finally receives its customary reward and the girl emerges. Avendaño is struck dumb by what he considers to be the lovely, almost angelic, vision before him. We are told nothing about her appearance except that she is "vestida como labradora" and carrying a candle (241). The muleteer had, of course, given his version of her beauty but it is Avendaño's personal reaction that is now important and we are influenced by what "le parecía ver" (241). But the angelic vision fades away for us when Costanza abruptly questions the gaping Avendaño. Not so for him. He replies in a polite, rather stilted sentence which she at once turns to ridicule: "Vaya, hermano, norabuena . . ." (241). The angel is a bit surly; the girl's beauty is not reflected in her words. Avendaño's idealised view of Costanza is contrasted, in our opinion, by the reality of her approach to him. She leaves the room and the effect of her departure on Avendaño "fue . . . lo que suele ser al caminante ponerse el sol y sobrevenir la noche lóbrega y escura" (242). We recall the previous reference to the onset of the night. Here, however, we are not confronted with a humorous contrast contained within the sentence. Humour is, indeed, present but it stems from the contrast between the pompous description of her departure and its actual purpose: to arrange for the provision of clean sheets for the boys' beds. We see, too, that despite her abruptness she is still on the pedestal of Avendaño's admiration. For these are, in fact, the words he might use to describe her exit. Avendaño is now utterly lovesick for, when they go for a meal, "Carriazo cenó lo que le dieron y Avendaño lo que con él llevaba, que fueron pensamientos e imaginaciones" (243). Again balance and again, apparently, a contrast. But, is it really a contrast? Is not Avendaño's present state somewhat similar to that of Carriazo earlier when he was "melancólico e imaginativo" (229)? Our suspicions in this respect are confirmed by an argument between the two boys when Carriazo criticises Avendaño for his undignified love of a kitchen maid. Avendaño's retort shows that the same criticism can be made of Carriazo's attraction to the wharves. The two objects of affection are thus equated, a situation which is underlined by the balance of "yo me iré con mi almadraba, y tú te quedarás con tu fregona" (246).

Avendaño's idealised view of Costanza is crystallised, to his displeasure, in a sonnet sung to her by a local suitor (247). Preciosa's poems come to our minds. We are conscious of the fact that it is a little incongruous to address a serving maid in this elaborate fashion and the fact that Costanza is sleeping like a log while her virtues are thus extolled adds a nice touch of humour (248). Avendaño, the idealistic lover, has to come to terms with the reality of his situation and accepts a job as a stable-boy in order to remain near his beloved. His plans for the conquest of Costanza are temporarily shelved by Cervantes when he turns his attention to the adventures and misadventures of Carriazo, the newly-fledged water-carrier, a job he has acquired in order to remain near his friend Avendaño. During this time Avendaño, although unable to make any progress with Costanza, becomes more in love with her than ever for she, in his opinion, "no menos enamora con su recogimiento que con su hermosura" (264). Carriazo mocks his persistence and solemnity, laughingly equating Costanza with historical and mythological heroines. This, too, is a form of idealisation but not one that Avendaño accepts because it does not stem from love as does his. He now launches into a lengthy description of the effect love has on him and the way in which it transforms the reality of Costanza's position into something fantastic and elevated. The language he uses is often pedantic and elaborate: "encumbrar", "alguna mina de gran valor", "un breve término" (265). The sentences are longer than those he normally uses and their structure is more complex —take, for example, "que viéndole, no le vea, y conociéndole, le desconozca" or the parenthetical statements in the sentence beginning: "No es posible que . . ." (265). In all, a clear example of the high style mentioned in the Introduction. Appropriate if seen from Avendaño's point of view, but inappropriate if we concentrate on the reality of Costanza's status. Ana María Barrenechea, when discussing this declaration of love, claims that: "Cervantes lo expresa en uno de los pasajes de mayor sencillez y emoción que el amor le ha inspirado."[11]   Although we are made clearly aware of the sincerity and emotion of Avendaño, Cervantes hardly appears to have aimed at or achieved simplicity on this particular occasion.   Furthermore, Carriazo, "como exclamando," uses the same type of language and style, first to comment on this virtuous love and then to address his own neglected tunny fish (265-66).   By this similarity of language and the juxtaposition of Costanza and the fish he intends to mock Avendaño's adoration. But, as we are always mindful of the fact that he is, in many ways, as much in love as his friend, we are conscious of an element of truth in his description of himself as "tan enamorado y aficionado vuestro" (266). Cervantes is here using the high style specifically as a means of making us laugh   —using it for something as humdrum as a fish. And in a moment the two lapse back into their normal manner of speaking (266-67).   The pompous lover becomes the argumentative friend. It is this swift changeover from one style to another which provides one of the most important and attractive features of his work.

The lively song which Carriazo improvises about the other servants in the inn is in many ways a parody poem, at times bordering on the nonsensical and saying virtually nothing. It is followed almost immediately by a song from one of Costanza's admirers in the same verse form, though without a refrain. This is, however, the only similarity between the two poems since they are poles apart in style and content. The whole of the second poem is riddled with hyperbole, presenting a series of exaggerations, which centre chiefly upon the equation of Costanza with all the various elements of the heavens. The overall effect is one of pedantry, and the poem is not even redeemed by musicality such as was found in the songs addressed to Preciosa. Here we have high style at its peak or, one feels tempted to say, at its worst.

[11] Ana María Barrenechea, '*La ilustre fregona* como ejemplo de estructura novelesca cervantina', *Actas del primer congreso internacional de hispanistas* (Oxford, 1964), p. 201.

The emptiness is apparent and there is little emotion to redeem it. The moment the song ends a couple of chunks of brick crash down at the feet of the performer who consequently makes a hurried and ignominious exit. Cervantes could hardly have thought of a more effective manner of deflating the high style. But he is not finished with it even yet. The servant, Barrabás, who has earlier objected to a description which he misunderstood in Carriazo's song (269), now presents his critical judgement on this poem. In brief, he feels the language of the song is inappropriate. A serving maid should not be described in such celestial language. He suggests a lot of down-to-earth comparisons which would be much more fitting. We immediately notice that they are also much more meaningful and far more vivid than the ones in the original poem, for "stiff as asparagus, as white as milk, harder than a lump of mortar"are the descriptions proffered by Barrabás (276). We recall the first description of Costanza (238-39), that of the muleteer, where the language is a mixture of straightforward, natural comparisons ("áspera como una ortiga") and more stylised expressions ("en una mejilla tiene el sol, y en la otra, la luna; la una es hecha de rosas, y la otra de claveles"). But here, too, the simplicity which Barrabás advocates, dominates. His commentary on the poem underlines for us how empty the high style often is.

This refined expression of love is soon contrasted with the coarse overtures of two serving maids, la Argüello and la Gallega, to the two boys. They consider themselves as good as high-class ladies, claiming "venimos hechas unas archiduquesas" (278). But through a single word Cervantes puts them in their proper place when instead of "poniendo la nariz por el agujero" he writes "poniendo los hocicos" (278). The intrusion of the animal world neatly sums them up. When we recall his analysis of the rôle of Juana Carducha in *La gitanilla* it is not surprising to find Casalduero describing these two wenches as "el asedio que el amor lascivo prepara tanto para Carriazo como para

Avendaño" (*Sentido y forma,* p. 196). An interesting detail is high-lighted by Ana María Barrenechea when she points out that: "Primero ha dicho [Cervantes] que se volvieron 'tristes y malaventuradas a sus lechos' y luego repite con ligera variación 'a su triste cama' . . . Con el cambio de lugar de un adjetivo resume su pobre soledad en una suprema manifestación de su capacidad de compasión" ('*La ilustre fregona* como ejemplo de estructura', pp. 204-5). This is not an aspect which Cervantes develops in his portrayal of them. Nor does he present them as Lust personified. The impression they create is chiefly one of foolish impertinence, lacking in both *honestidad* and *discreción.*

Avendaño, meanwhile, has been ruminating in the background and has succeeded in composing his own set of verses in honour of Costanza. Again the high style is obvious in the choice of words and the tortuous construction of the sentences (281-82). Such a poem should indeed be carefully inscribed on fine parchment; Avendaño had jotted it down in his barley ledger. This contrast between the poem and the place in which it is recorded serves to remind us of the continuing one between the idealising nature of Avendaño's love and its lowly object. In addition, a comic and contrasting framework is provided by the arguments and discussion of the innkeeper and his wife.

Under the guise of a cure for toothache a piece of paper declaring Avendaño's love and real social status reaches Costanza's hands. He conveniently twists the facts to suit his purpose, claiming that he left home because of the fame of her beauty. This would be the conventional situation. The fact that a chance encounter, after he had already left home, encouraged him to come to the inn does not present quite such a flattering situation. Costanza takes the paper away, and as Avendaño waits "le estuvo palpitando el corazón, temiendo y esperando, o ya la sentencia de su muerte, o la restauración de su vida" (286). A tense moment when we see it through Avendaño's eyes. The language is, once again, that which he would have selected. And how does Costanza react? The precious paper is torn to shreds.

The remaining episodes of the story deal chiefly with Carriazo's adventures and the lengthy revelation of Costanza's real identity. As in *La gitanilla* the finale consists of marriage. Here, in fact, we have three weddings: Avendaño and Costanza, Carriazo and the *Corregidor*'s daughter, don Pedro (son of the *Corregidor* and unlucky suitor of Costanza) and Avendaño's sister. "Desta manera quedaron todos contentos, alegres y satisfechos" (323). There is, of course, nothing unusual in pairing off all those eligible at the end of a story or play. The fact that Carriazo has not been courting the *Corregidor*'s daughter and that we know virtually nothing about his bride-to-be is irrelevant. Looked at from one standpoint the marriages, which promise to be happy ones, are a form of reward. Avendaño, like Andrés, is rewarded for his virtuous love of a girl he thought was really his social inferior; Carriazo gets a prize for his faithful friendship; and don Pedro's betrothal is compensation for his failure to win Costanza and an acknowledgement of the fact that there was nothing dishonourable in his love. More pertinently at this juncture we can see that the marriages, particularly those of Carriazo and Avendaño, create an effective ending because it is a balanced one. The puzzling antithesis of *ilustre fregona* has been resolved, and the frequently antithetical portrayal of these two lads now culminates in their marriages. But, as we saw earlier, the word 'antithetical' conveys only one aspect of the situation since Cervantes makes us aware, too, of the great similarity between the two boys. The objects of their affection are completely dissimilar, yet the attitudes of the two youths are often identical. This equation is frequently brought about by the use of similar adjectives or expressions and by the fact that in many respects they both have an idealistic approach. As we have seen, the high style is employed to convey this aspect through both prose and poetry. The same tendency was found in *La gitanilla*, particularly in the songs addressed to Preciosa. There we accepted them, appreciating the serious intention behind them, and if the incongruity between them and the status of the person addressed did occur to us we could easily account for it. The effect caused in *La ilustre fregona* is entirely different. We laugh at the pompous poems, we smile when Avendaño's toothache cure is rejected. And this effect is a calculated one, arising from Cervantes' skilful juxtaposition of ideal and real, of high style and low style, of inflated attitudes and deflating incidents. The low style was traditionally the one used to make people laugh; here Cervantes uses both low and high to achieve this result. The zigzagging course between one style and the other, the speed of the changeover and the balanced presentation of contrasts add up to an aesthetically satisfying *novela.*

The terms 'reality' and 'real' have been used rather loosely in the above commentary. How genuine is the reality that Cervantes here presents? He does indeed begin by rooting the story in reality: "En Burgos . . ." Pick up an English text which begins "In York, a few years ago . . ." and you start prepared for at least the possibility of a realistic portrayal. The names of the two families probably mean nothing to us and it is unlikely that even the readers of Cervantes' day would have been acquainted with the facts unearthed by Blanca de los Ríos, namely that these two surnames appear on the matriculation register for the University of Salamanca (the boys' ostensible destination) for the three years 1581-4 and also that a magistrate called Carriazo held office in Burgos in 1569 and 1570. These details are recorded by Amezúa y Mayo, *Cervantes, creador,* II, pp. 295-6. Although the discovery of these data might suggest that Cervantes was dealing with real people and actual experiences, this is not made apparent to us in the opening paragraph. We might possibly have expected that the presentation of the picaresque life on the fishing wharves would be used by Cervantes to form a realistic contrast to the idealistic aspect of the story. In fact, since his portrayal of this potentially seamy side of life is based chiefly on Carriazo's attitudes to it, we tend to see it through the rose-coloured distorting lenses of the latter's spectacles. Life in an inn also opens up the opportunity for an author to dwell on the realities of existence. But, once again, Cervantes has failed to exploit this possible development. Life below stairs is portrayed vividly, particularly in la Gallega and la Argüello, but none of this can be neatly labelled 'Realism'. What we have is a semblance of reality carefully created, engineered even, by Cervantes in order to contrast with the idealistic aspects of his *novela*. In other words, he has taken such standard, conventional facets of reality as food, coarse manners, and work, and has artistically integrated them into his *novela* at the appropriate junctures, in order to bring out the contrasts and comparisons which are so much part of our enjoyment of this work; it is hardly necessary to add that this created reality itself seems to us more real by this same juxtaposition. Ana María Barrenechea warns against the temptation of seeing "la novela partida en dos mundos: ideal (Avendaño y Costanza), real (Carriazo, criados, mozos de mulas etc.), inverosímil-verosímil, noble-bajo" ('*La ilustre fregona* como ejemplo de estructura', p. 203). As we have seen, all these facets do exist but they are not mutually exclusive. Nor is Cervantes supporting one at the expense of the other. Both 'worlds' are vital to the concept and presentation of the *novela* and the constant shifting of emphasis, the frequent transposition of features from one to the other are important and meaningful.

Those who do stress the realism of the *novela* tend to be somewhat disconcerted by the incredible coincidences towards the end of the story. Costanza's long-lost father arrives conveniently just after the *Corregidor* (and the readers) have been told the inn-keeper's side of her story. Then, rather irrelevantly too, Avendaño's father turns out to be related to the *Corregidor*. Finally, there are fortunately two spare, eligible girls to enable a trio of marriages to take place. Hardly realistic: indeed, almost unrealistic. However, we must remember that if we find it hard to swallow such coincidences they were probably easily digested by Cervantes' contemporaries for whom they would be part of the stock-in-trade of literature. We, too, should try and visualize them chiefly as part of the dramatic structure which Cervantes is using to convey attitudes and ideas. But if such an approach is still unpalatable various examples of effective description and even of penetrating psychology can be found to compensate for the artificial coincidences. The rôle played by the boys' *ayo*, who is to accompany them to Salamanca, is an insignificant one. But this does not mean that Cervantes gives him second-class treatment. On the contrary, he brings him to life, albeit for but a short period, with the delightful comment that "se había dejado crecer la barba, porque diese autoridad a su cargo" (231). Further evidence of Cervantes' understanding of the human mind is shown by his remark that a visit from the police makes even the innocent feel guilty (296). And the fact that Carriazo's generosity in giving back the money he won in gambling is forgotten while the farcical episode of the tail is remembered clearly points also to a recognisable human tendency (294). The innkeeper's offer of help when Carriazo is in jail is a monstrous and amusing version of the 'friend-of-a-friend' type of operation (260-61), exaggerated beyond measure but still containing a seed of truth within it. The nice, practical details about the non-availability of meals in the inn (243) and the detailed picture of Costanza's clothes (249-51), though very different, can also contribute to a catalogue of redeeming features for those who require one. It is to aspects such as these that we can best apply the comment of Amezúa y Mayo: "En *La ilustre fregona* es la facultad observadora de Cervantes la que triunfa" (*Cervantes, creador*, II, p. 310). Yet we must still bear in mind that creative interpretation is equally important.

As with *La gitanilla* the *ejemplaridad* of the *novela* must also be determined. The most obvious starting-point is Costanza. Yet as soon as we do begin to concentrate on her we find that there is very little on which to focus. As Ana María Barrenechea points out, she is "un personaje en hueco, que el lector sólo conoce a través de los otros personajes por el influjo que ejerce en ellos" ('*La ilustre fregona* como ejemplo de estructura', p. 200). If we place her beside Preciosa she will probably appear merely a weak, shadowy maiden with a pretty face and a sharp tongue. And it must be added that this tongue is found in action on only eight brief occasions. Preciosa's lengthy speeches revealing her *discreción* and *honestidad*, her wit and her powers of reasoning are never part of Costanza's programme. All the same, it is beside Preciosa that her place is to be found. Like Preciosa, Costanza has been reared in an environment which could easily have had a corrupting influence upon her. The *pellizco* that the young muleteer claimed to have given her is indicative of the type of behaviour with which she would frequently be in contact (238). It does not need much imagination on our part to visualise the siting of such a pinch. Costanza reacted to it by slapping its originator across the face. It all seems very crude and far removed from the wordy exchanges of *La gitanilla* yet it is a graphic portrayal of the same sort of situation which Preciosa often encountered. In her violent rejection of the muleteer's advances Costanza is, in fact, proving her *honestidad* and *discreción*. These qualities are all the more apparent when we compare her attitude with that of la Gallega and la Argüello who, one imagines, could never have a surfeit of pinches. They are keen to take advantage of every opportunity for new conquests offered by life in the inn. Moreover they, like Juana Carducha, take the initiative in a most unladylike fashion. Costanza not only keeps herself aloof from all physical advances, but also turns a deaf ear and an unreceptive heart to more refined expressions of love as found in the serenades. She accepted Avendaño's epistle simply because she believed it to be a prayer guaranteed to cure toothache and settled down to read it "con mucho gusto y más devoción" (285). On discovering she had been tricked into reading a declaration of love, she reacted violently. In addition to being such a prudent maiden where love is concerned she is also shown to be a dutiful daughter to those she believes to be her parents. As in the case of Preciosa the ultimate revelation of her real identity and social status are to be considered a tribute to and a proof of the way in which she has behaved. Despite the truth of all these assertions one feels bound to admit that Costanza is really a rather negative sort of character. We can say she is virtuous, prudent and dutiful simply because she refuses to let herself get involved. There is little that is actively virtuous about her. For much of the time she is safely closeted in a back-room of the inn, presumably devoting all her loving care to producing a good shine on the silver. This is not, of course, to say that if she were really tempted she would succumb but to indicate that she is not such a satisfying artistic creation as Preciosa.

Nonetheless Costanza is undeniably *ejemplar*. But, like Preciosa, she is not the only source of *ejemplaridad* in the story. At the beginning of the *novela* Cervantes explains to us in great detail Carriazo's motivation for his first picaresque escapade. In fact, the word 'escapade' adequately sums it up, for Carriazo, "llevado de una inclinación picaresca, sin forzarle a ello algún mal tratamiento que sus padres le hiciesen, sólo por su gusto y antojo, se desgarró . . . de casa de sus padres" (221-22). If it were not for the presence of the adjective *picaresca* we should probably not suspect that this is the sort of society Carriazo is going to join. As it is, the term loses most of its value through being attached to the noun *inclinación*. A person either was or was not a *pícaro*; to be prompted to action by an "inclinación picaresca" was an artificial, half-way stage. In addition, the circumstances are not those of a genuine *pícaro*. Carriazo has well-to-do parents who do not beat him. The right premises for a picaresque novel are thus lacking. What Carriazo wants to do is to play truant from home to enjoy "la vida libre" (222) which appears to be a welcome change from the restrictions of civilisation. Because this life is the result of choice and not of necessity it appears to him as ideal in every respect. Things that a real unwilling *pícaro* would have considered a hardship he finds a source of pleasure (222). He indulges in all of them and is so enthusiastic in his practical study of the picaresque life that he becomes a real authority on it. But just as Cervantes had made clear the motives for Carriazo's departure from home so, too, he now shows us that despite all his newly acquired accomplishments no really radical change is effected in Carriazo's character. His generous behaviour towards his mates gives proof of his good breeding and he is, in fact, presented as the antithesis of a genuine *pícaro* for he is "virtuoso, limpio, bien criado y . . . discreto" (224). Because his choice of the picaresque life was a voluntary one he is able to leave it at will, and, suitably attired, return to his family. Since he continues to have such an idealised view of life on the fishing wharves he is easily able to persuade Avendaño to join him on his next excursion. We are able to appreciate the irony of the emotional farewell scene as the two lads set off, ostensibly for glorious careers at the University (231). We wait, expectantly, to see how they are going to manage to escape from the *ayo* and what they will do when they reach the wharves. But neither of them ever gets there because, as we have seen, they chance to hear the muleteer's description of Costanza. But this is clearly an over-simplification. The description is part of the mechanics of the plot; Avendaño fails to reach the wharves because he is rooted in Toledo by his love for Costanza. We have already seen how idealising that love is and how it often created a humorous contrast with the reality of the circumstances. But it is essential to realize that we never actually laugh *at* Avendaño. We cannot fail to appreciate the sincerity, the nobility of his love even though we may be unable entirely to comprehend his enthusiasm for the comparatively silent Costanza. His love is for him an ideal, a worthy good towards which he can strive. Carriazo, although recognising that the girl is beautiful, does not feel the same compulsion to delay their projected visit. His love for the wharves tugs at his heart. But we notice that he does not forge ahead with his own plans but hangs around with Avendaño, albeit rather unwillingly. When the latter obtains employment in the inn Carriazo also gets a job, for "no quiso él quedarse a buenas noches, y más, que consideró el gran gusto que haría a Avendaño si le seguía el humor" (253). We have here a somewhat apologetic description of friendship for it is, basically, this that prevents Carriazo from going off on his own.

Thus the two lads abandon their jaunt to the fishing wharves. Because of two noble emotions, love on the part of one of them and friendship on the part of the other, they are saved from a life which, however attractive it might be to them on the surface, would ultimately be a degrading one. Moreover, while in the inn, although acting as servants, they both maintain standards in keeping with their upbringing and characters. They repulse la Argüello and la Gallega; Carriazo, as in his initial escapade, proves to be "bien nacido . . . liberal y compasivo" when handing back to the loser the money he won when gambling (293). Casalduero, however, finds little to commend in the behaviour of Carriazo, particularly when compared with that of his half-sister Costanza: "La muchacha, hija del desmán paterno, vive en la libertad del mesón una vida virtuosa y ejemplar; el muchacho, fruto de la unión legal y legítima, se ha lanzado a la picaresca en busca de un nivel natural que le aleje de toda disciplina y de todo orden . . . Va de pendencia en pendencia, y siempre en manos de la justicia, se hace famoso en la ciudad por su apelativo indecente" (*Sentido y forma*, p. 199). Casalduero has disregarded the good points enumerated by Cervantes and has somewhat distorted the element of youthful abandon. Because they stay in the inn they are discovered by their fathers. Now, at first sight this is not an event which seems likely to appeal to them. They are ashamed and annoyed at being spotted. But because of all the attendant circumstances this discovery produces not their chastisement but a reward. Any chance of their immersion in the picaresque life is now completely ruled out. The little tableau in which Avendaño and his father are reunited and reconciled is likened to the return of the Prodigal Son. The causes of the two situations are different but the effects the same (321). The fact that the boys' escapade is definitely over and done with is underlined by their marriages. The youthful desire for freedom has been superseded by respectable social conformity. The story ends in Burgos, where it began. It ends, moreover, with the stress on the family unit which was also its starting point. It is recorded that Carriazo has three sons who, oblivious of the fact that there are such things as fishing wharves, are now students in Salamanca, the University to which their father claimed he was going. The apparently wayward youth has, as far as we can tell, become a good father and a respectable citizen. We must remember, too, that about sixteen years previously Carriazo senior had also demonstrated a different type of irresponsibility when he raped Costanza's mother, an act for which he has now made amends through his search for Costanza and his admission of his lax behaviour.

In the course of the *novela* Cervantes suggests that Carriazo's behaviour is typical of many youths of his social class for, referring to the wharves, he comments "allí van, o envían, muchos padres principales a buscar a sus hijos, y los hallan; y tanto sienten sacarlos de aquella vida como si los llevaran a dar muerte" (226-27). We should not necessarily take this at its face value and imagine there was a full-scale exodus of mildly angry young men heading for the wharves. What it does indicate to us is that Cervantes was well aware of the need of many youngsters to escape from the life and standards inherited from their parents. Cervantes is not actually praising Carriazo's specific course of action which, on one occasion, he describes as "baja determinación" (230). However, boys will be boys. Indeed, boys should be boys. The suggestion is that it is advisable for them to get it out of their system while they are still free from responsibilities. Cervantes also makes it clear to us that he considers this is just a temporary phase in the life of an individual. Youthful rebelliousness does not necessarily imply an erring adult. One might have thought that this tendency, found first in Carriazo senior and then in his son, would be reflected also in the latter's children. If this had been the case we should have been able to visualise their lives unfolding, with them, too, having a youthful fling before arriving at stability. Such a sense of repetition would have been effective. However, the ending Cervantes has given us is far more meaningful, for the serious-minded student sons are intended as a vivid illustration of the fact that no permanent damage has been done either to Carriazo in particular or to society in general by his youthful outburst. Boys will be boys. All's well that ends well. It is interesting to recall at this point that the three years that Carriazo spent on the wharves were profitably employed by Avendaño studying at Salamanca, "por su gusto" (230). He never had any personal "inclinación picaresca" but was enticed from his studies by Carriazo's enthusiasm for adventure. Nor did he ever become a *pícaro*. The younger generation, currently at Salamanca, appear to be following the pattern of his life rather than adopting the rebelliousness of their father. Casalduero feels that the final emphasis is placed on Carriazo's situation: "se casa, tiene hijos, es feliz; pero vive temiendo" (*Sentido y forma*, p. 200). This fear is based on his belief that sooner or later he will be reminded of the farcical episode of the tail of the ass. He is, therefore, unable to escape the consequences of his past behaviour. This is, indeed, to suggest a grim *ejemplo*.

In laying the stress on the rôle of Carriazo one must not forget that it is in actual fact Avendaño who puts the first spoke in their picaresque wheel, as we have already seen. But this does not in any way weaken the impact of Cervantes' ideas on youthful behaviour. Although we have been able to see many instances in which the two boys appeared dramatically opposed we have also seen that, fundamentally, they have many traits in common. When Avendaño is kept in Toledo by love of Costanza, his ideal, this is more than a mere dramatic device. Cervantes is showing us that ideals have a strong pull. Although it is Avendaño who is overcome by love of Costanza, Carriazo, as we have seen, is included in the effects of the love because of his concept of friendship.

This *novela ejemplar* presents not so much a moral as an encouraging statement about human nature. The basic statement is, moreover, one which is equally relevant here and now. This is undeniably intended by Cervantes as a serious comment but it must not leave us with the impression that the mirth and the farcical elements are therefore out of place or mere gimmicks. Our laughter is caused chiefly by the many contrasts; it is these contrasts which lead us to see in the first instance what Cervantes is aiming at in his story. In *La gitanilla* humour was produced by individual incidents and details; in *La ilustre fregona* it is fundamental to the whole concept and presentation of the story. As in *La gitanilla* Cervantes has here used clichés of language, situation and technique but he has used them as a means to an end. In many instances the use he makes of them could be called revolutionary. A revolution often produces deaths; Cervantes', on the contrary, gave new life to the *novela*.

IV

Conclusion

The most obvious question to ask on coming to the end of a study of these two *novelas* is: How typical are they of the collection as a whole? Yet at the same time it is an almost unanswerable question since the 'typical' Cervantine *novela* exists only in the imagination. Certainly there are frequent affinities of atmosphere, story, style or moral but these do not add up to a blueprint for the *novela*. When examining the two stories we have seen to what extent they can be considered good tales, providing the pleasure Cervantes said was his intention, and also how they fulfilled his aim of conveying "algún ejemplo provechoso". Such an analysis could be made of the remaining *novelas* but one would constantly be aware of their individuality as much as of their similarity.

Another line of approach is more satisfactory: What impression do we receive of Cervantes, as artist and man, from these two *novelas* and how characteristic is such an impression? As we have seen, the stories are a medley of convention and originality. The conventional aspect is to be found chiefly in his inclusion of many of the standard literary features of his day. We have the concealed-identity type of story, beautiful heroines, they-all-lived-happily-ever-after endings and glimpses of the picaresque. The accepted topics of jealousy, disdain, love (with overtones of the courtly variety) all duly make their appearance. Cervantes was well acquainted with his literary heritage and shows no inclination to reject it out of hand. Often we wince at the clichés or groan at the coincidences. Yet it is in the inclusion of these same conventional features that his originality is often seen, since they are for him basically a means to an end. Jealousy in *La gitanilla* proves to be the means of revealing to us Andrés' progress; the stylised expression of Avendaño's love in *La ilustre fregona* is skilfully used in a series of comparisons and contrasts. When considered at their face value and in isolation such features will appear merely samples of the literary stock-in-trade, but when seen as an integral part of the story and in the light of Cervantes' purpose they take on new life and meaning. Cervantes has carefully exploited the literary tradition with which his readers would be well acquainted. He is speaking to them on a familiar wavelength —they would know all about the ins and outs of jealousy, marriages would be highly acceptable— so they would, then, be tuned in to receive Cervantes' interpretation of the situations contained in his story. This is something he does time and time again in these *novelas*: conventional material presented with an original twist or a new interpretation. And, of course, the most obvious example of Cervantes' skill in this respect is the use made in *Don Quijote* of the chivalresque material.

His originality is to be found, too, in the numerous little details we have noticed —details which, while irrelevant for the story and its meaning, often bring a character to life momentarily or make a scene easier for us to visualize. One tends to suspect that these details usually emerge from Cervantes' observation of human behaviour. Their inclusion is part of his creative skill and certainly makes for a good author-reader relationship. When reading the chivalresque or the pastoral one often seems to be viewing the story at a distance, as if it were being acted out on a lofty stage. With these two *novelas,* although we are aware of the chronological and geographical gap, we are much more able to enter into the story —it is taking place on our level. And this different reaction is due in no small part to the presence of these revealing details. Again, this is far from being an exclusive quality of these two *novelas* or even of the collection in general. Examples abound in *Don Quijote* and are to be found, too, in the more rarefied atmosphere of the *Persiles.*

With regard to the ideas and attitudes expressed by Cervantes through these two stories the most noticeable trait is his common sense. The medium through which he conveys his views may be exaggerated or fanciful but what he is actually saying is very sound. Cervantes has his feet firmly on the ground. Moreover, it is through his ideas that another aspect of his originality is often seen, for they are far from being stereotyped. His ideas are workable ones; not purely academic. In these two texts what he says about marriage, about the effects of love, about youthful behaviour, about the rôle of parents suggests to us that he was a keen student of man in society. Even though the actual characterisation is not very developed the basic human traits that he presents are recognisable ones. The fact that the characterisation may appear very shallow to the modern reader is not to be considered as indicative of an artistic failing on the part of Cervantes. He never intended to present his heroes and heroines in depth with all aspects of their psychological and emotional make-up carefully graded. Having provided them with sufficient traits to make them appear as individuals he then concentrated on the meaning that he wished to convey through them. We can see that it would be preposterous to attempt a character analysis of Costanza and, although Preciosa is given much fuller treatment, it would be equally non-productive to subject her to a similar process. It is, indeed, indicative of Cervantes' talent that he can convey so many varied aspects of human nature without employing detailed character studies. In addition, he often pinpoints the complexities of human relationships, the way in which a person's behaviour depends upon that of the people with whom he comes in contact. It is seventeenth-century Spanish society that he is describing but since human nature provides so much of his material the resulting implications are universal and atemporal. This, too, is applicable to a large section of his work: strip away the purely local aspects and the basic truth is seen to be relevant to the present day. This fact has, of course, meant that each century, each generation even, has tended to see its own image reflected in many of Cervantes' works, to interpret them according to its own beliefs and standards. The countless books of criticism on *Don Quijote* in particular bear witness to this. For each age the figure of Don Quijote has signified something different. This is not in itself reprehensible so long as such specialised interpretations do not blind us to Cervantes' own intentions. Such books of criticism often reveal more about their authors and the time at which they were written than about Cervantes' masterpiece. But it is a tribute to Cervantes' skill that his work can be considered, not just as an example of a certain type of literature written at a certain period of history, but as something with continuing relevance.

Another aspect of Cervantes himself which is disclosed over and over again in these stories is his humour —not the joking sort but usually subtle, sly comments, often presented in a very straightfaced manner. We have noted numerous examples of this. It is not just to add entertainment value, nor to jolly along his readers; it is usually an integral part of Cervantes' vision and presentation of humans. People are basically odd and amusing. Even in the *novela* of *El celoso extremeño* laughter is often produced by his depiction of the characters within this tragic set-up. The reader who can get through the majority of the chapters of *Don Quijote* without laughing must be rare indeed. And, like so many other aspects of his work, the humour does not really date.

In his prologue to the *Novelas ejemplares* Cervantes wrote: "Mi intento ha sido poner en la plaza de nuestra república una mesa de trucos, donde cada uno pueda llegar a entretenerse sin daño de barras; digo sin daño del alma ni del cuerpo, porque los ejercicios honestos y agradables antes aprovechan que dañan." When equating his *novelas* with a harmless game of billiards, providing relaxation and healthy exercise, Cervantes was clearly under-rating them. For we have discovered not only the pleasure and profit which can be derived from reading them but also the profound statements that Cervantes is making about humans, about us.

Bibliographical Note

1. *The Chivalresque Novel*

Auerbach, Erich. *Mimesis: the Representation of Reality in Western Literature*. Princeton, 1957; first published 1951. Chapter 6 deals with aspects of reality in the chivalresque novel.

Dronke, Peter. *Medieval Latin and the Rise of European Love Lyric*. Vol. I, Oxford, 1965. An examination of the source, nature and diffusion of some of the facets of courtly love.

Lewis, C. S. *The Allegory of Love*. Oxford, 1958; first published 1936. A study of courtly love in society and literature.

Vinaver, Eugène. *Form and Meaning in Medieval Romance*. The Presidential Address of the Modern Humanities Research Association, 1966. An interesting and illuminating essay on the structure of the chivalresque romance.

2. *The Pastoral Novel*

Avalle-Arce, J. B. *La novela pastoril española*. Madrid, 1959. An important study of the development of the genre in Spain, with chapters devoted to the *Diana, Diana enamorada* and Cervantes.

Solé-Leris, A. 'The theory of love in the two *Dianas:* a contrast.' *Bulletin of Hispanic Studies*, XXXVI (1959), 65-79. A detailed examination of the rôle of love in these two novels.

Wardropper, B. W. 'The *Diana:* revaluation and interpretation.' *Studies in Philology*, XLVIII (1951), 126-144. A thorough analysis of Montemayor's *Diana*.

3. *The Picaresque Novel*

Parker, A. A. *Literature and the Delinquent*. Edinburgh, 1967. An excellent and eminently readable study of the background and growth of the picaresque novel in Spain and Europe, 1599-1753.

4. *Cervantes: Editions*

The edition which has been followed for the study of *La gitanilla* and *La ilustre fregona* is that of Francisco Rodríguez Marín for the Clásicos Castellanos series: *Novelas ejemplares*, I, Madrid, 1969; the first edition appeared in 1915. It does not contain Cervantes' *Prólogo al lector* which can be found in *Novelas ejemplares*, I, ed. Schevill and Bonilla, Madrid, 1922.

5. *Cervantes: General*

Arco y Garay, R. *La sociedad española en las obras de Cervantes*. Madrid, 1951. A catalogue of the aspects of contemporary society revealed in Cervantes' works.

Entwistle, W. J. *Cervantes.* Oxford, 1940. A general study of Cervantes' life and works.

Riley, E. C. *Cervantes's Theory of the Novel.* Oxford,1962. A profound and stimulating book, basic to an understanding of Cervantes' concept of literature.

6. *Cervantes: Las novelas ejemplares*

Casalduero, Joaquín. *Sentido y forma de las 'Novelas ejemplares'.* Buenos Aires, 1943. A study of the individual *novelas,* often stressing their spiritual implications.

Castro, Américo. 'La ejemplaridad de las novelas cervantinas.' *Nueva Revista de Filología Hispánica,* II (1948), 319-332. A somewhat biased analysis of the presence or absence of *ejemplaridad* in the stories.

Entwistle, W. J. 'Cervantes, the exemplary novelist.' *Hispanic Review,* IX (1941), 103-109. A brief attempt at determining the exemplary quality of various *novelas.*

González de Amezúa y Mayo, A. *Cervantes, creador de la novela corta española.* Two vols, Madrid, 1958. The first volume is devoted to a study of the antecedents and development of the *novela.* Volume II contains a commentary on each of the stories in the collection and refers to their subsequent translation or adaptation.

Pierce, Frank. 'Reality and realism in the Exemplary Novels.' *Bulletin of Hispanic Studies,* XXX (1953), 134-142. A discussion of the various levels of existence found in some of the *novelas,* with particular reference to *La gitanilla* and *La ilustre fregona.*

7. *Cervantes: La gitanilla*

Forcione, Alban K. *Cervantes, Aristotle and the 'Persiles'.* Princeton, 1970. The section 'The poet as an outsider: *La gitanilla*' (306-319) analyses in depth the rôles of Preciosa and Clemente.

8. *Cervantes: La ilustre fregona*

Barrenechea, Ana María. '*La ilustre fregona* como ejemplo de estructura novelística cervantina.' *Actas del primer congreso internacional de hispanistas,* Oxford, 1964, 199-206. A fairly close textual study of the main aspects and effects of antithesis in this *novela.*

Blanco Aguinaga, C. 'Cervantes y la picaresca.' *Nueva Revista de Filología Hispánica,* XI (1957), 313-342. The article includes a discussion of this element in *La ilustre fregona.*